Praise for *Must-Win Battles*

"This is a great book because it addresses the issues increasingly faced by corporations in a global economy; without emotional buy-in from the people within the organization, it is extremely difficult to deliver superior performance. It is no longer enough to have the best strategy, technology or assets. Total emotional buy-in will provide the differentiator."
**Gautam Thapar, Vice Chairman and Managing Director,
Ballarpur Industries Limited**

"Management teams usually know what needs to be done, but many struggle to act on this knowledge. This book defines a clear pathway to overcome the blockages created when managers either do not know how to get implementation started or are apprehensive about engaging on very difficult issues with their teams. If you are looking for tools to help you win your must-win battles, this is the book you need."
Larry Pillard, Chairman of the Board of Directors, Tetra Laval Group

"This book provides real insight to the leader who is faced with having to very rapidly determine a clear set of priorities and then act upon them. *Must-Win Battles* is a practical guide in determining those battles that simply have to be addressed and won emotionally and intellectually. A pity it wasn't around when I started!"
Tony Froggatt, CEO, Scottish & Newcastle PLC

"*Must-Win Battles* squarely addresses the real challenges that face executives every day. There are no clear-cut formulas to separate strategy, team and leadership development. They must be completey integrated. The must-win battle process, by recognizing this explicitly, has the potential to make a big difference in developing strategies that work in practice."
**Michael Y. Yoshino
Herman Krannert Professor of Business Administration, Emeritus
Harvard Business School**

"Anyone who has built a business knows that inspiring minds as well as inspiring ideas are what matters. Behind every success are people that are working as a team. *Must-Win Battles* offers practical insights for every business, no matter how big or small, into how to harness aspirations and energy to win the battles that really matter."
James Sanson, CEO, Computers Unlimited

"*Must-Win Battles* demonstrates the critical role that people play in delivering results and, hence, the critical importance of leadership and internal communications in galvanizing people not only to make successful strategies but also to realize them in practice."
Mark Read, Director of Strategy and Member of the Board, WPP PLC

FT Prentice Hall
FINANCIAL TIMES

In an increasingly competitive world, we believe it's quality of thinking that will give you the edge – an idea that opens new doors, a technique that solves a problem, or an insight that simply makes sense of it all. The more you know, the smarter and faster you can go.

That's why we work with the best minds in business and finance to bring cutting-edge thinking and best learning practice to a global market.

Under a range of leading imprints, including *Financial Times Prentice Hall*, we create world-class print publications and electronic products bringing our readers knowledge, skills and understanding, which can be applied whether studying or at work.

To find out more about Pearson Education publications, or tell us about the books you'd like to find, you can visit us at **www.pearsoned.co.uk**

PEARSON
Education

Must-win
battles™

Creating the focus you need to achieve your key business goals

Peter Killing ● Thomas Malnight ● with Tracey Keys

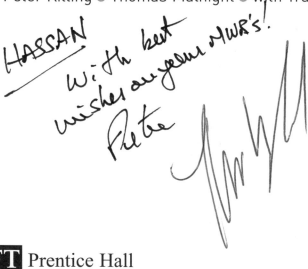

HASSAN

With best wishes on your MWB's!

Peter

FT Prentice Hall
FINANCIAL TIMES

An imprint of **Pearson Education**
Harlow, England • London • New York • Boston • San Francisco • Toronto • Sydney • Singapore • Hong Kong
Tokyo • Seoul • Taipei • New Delhi • Cape Town • Madrid • Mexico City • Amsterdam • Munich • Paris • Milan

Pearson Education Limited

Edinburgh Gate
Harlow CM20 2JE
tel: +44 (0)1279 623623
fax: +44 (0)1279 431059

First published in Great Britain in 2005

© Peter Killing, Thomas Malnight and Tracey Keys

The rights of Peter Killing, Thomas Malnight and Tracey Keys to be identified as authors of this work have been asserted by them in accordance with the Copyright, Designs and Patents Act 1988.

ISBN 0 273 70457 5

British Library Cataloguing in Publication Data
A catalogue record for this book is available from the British Library

Library of Congress Cataloging-in-Publication Data
A catalog record for this book is available from the Library of Congress

10 9 8 7 6 5 4 3 2 1
10 09 08 07 06 05

Typeset in Melior and Din by 70
Printed in Great Britain by Henry Ling Ltd, at the Dorset Press, Dorchester, Dorset

The publisher's policy is to use paper manufactured from sustainable forests.

contents

Why write this book?
(Or, who needs another management concept?)

Let's be clear. Although we are professors, we are not writing about some clever idea we have dreamed up and are hoping that some management team will try to then tell us whether it works. Nor did we "invent" the must-win battle® (MWB) concept and then unleash it on a collection of unsuspecting executives so we could write about the results.

In fact, the MWB idea evolved and developed over time as we worked with managers who were frustrated with their organizations' performance and wanted to drive real and sustainable change, while delivering concrete bottom-line impact. Consider some of the quotes you will come across later in this book – these are taken directly from senior managers before they embarked on their MWB journeys.

> We were a group of talented people, producing mediocre results. The potential to do much, much better was there.

> We had too many priorities – everything was important. Everyone was overwhelmed and heading in a different direction. It made no sense. It finally dawned on us – too many priorities meant no priorities.

> We had so-called priorities like "innovate more" which meant almost nothing. It was more a slogan than anything else. We needed to create real ownership of a few key priorities that would bring us the passion, focus, risk taking, and entrepreneurship that we needed. Business as usual would not get us there.

> We were too academic; we tried to make things perfect instead of making decisions. We were great at debates. Analysis drove out action.

We were a group of individuals in silos, not a team. There was no openness and even less trust. I had to break the prevailing mind set.

We were too internally focused, always talking about what we could and could not do. We need to concentrate on what we need to do to win in our markets and get on with it.

As we worked with these executives we began to realize that to dramatically increase the performance of their businesses, they needed to manage two things at once. First, they had to know how to identify and win the right battles. No question about that. No wins equals no positive results. But at the same time they had to be leading a much longer-term journey to create a more effective, less silo-based organization. They needed it if they were to win consistently the battles they engaged in. So that is why we call it the MWB journey. You are winning battles and transforming your organization at the same time.

And then came the first major debate. Should we, or should we not, combine intellectual thinking – hard strategy stuff – with the softer, more emotional elements of building a team into the same process? Some executives argued strongly no, others said yes, it is essential. And that is where we have come out.

Winning battles and transforming your organization both need to be built on the same truth: hard and soft must be combined. A great team without a sense of direction will go nowhere. A great strategy with no commitment will do no better. And without strong, authentic leadership, even both together are not sufficient. Many management books deal with one piece of the jigsaw or another. That's not good enough.

We have tried to fill the gap and show you that it can be done. We share what we have learned from many journeys, and while ours is still evolving, we hope that the insights will be useful to you.

Acknowledgments

We did not embark on this journey alone. Many people who have lived through the MWB experience generously shared with us their underlying thoughts – their public hopes, private fears, and tentative learnings – so that we could present an in-depth picture of what it means to lead such a journey. So our first thanks go to the many MWB participants we have worked with over the last few years, as their insights and experiences have provided the core elements of what you are about to read. We owe a special thanks to Kees van der Graaf of Unilever who has shared the personal story of his two-year MWB journey in Chapter 8.

IMD, our home institution, also deserves a special mention. This is a unique place. While being strongly focused on practical real-world experience and learning, it also supports research and writing, and without the generous research funding which has allowed Tracey Keys to devote long hours to this project, it never would have been completed. Our "no-holds-barred" colleagues at IMD have also provided a great sounding board for debating ideas, as well as some innovative concepts to augment our MWB toolkit.

On several MWB journeys we have worked with non-IMD colleagues, from whom we have learned much and shared the highs and lows that naturally come with the territory. Special thanks to Annie McKee and Fran Johnston of the Teleos Leadership Institute and to John Larrere and Sylvia DeVolge of the Hay Group. You contributed much to help shape the insights that are presented in this book.

Finally, without making this sound like an Oscar acceptance (we're not dressed for it anyway!), the encouragement and support of our families have been invaluable. From Tom, special thanks to Gabriela, Sophia,

Alexia, and Lukas, the joys of my life. From Peter, apologies and thanks to Rebecca for your willingness to put up with the many holidays that were not. And from Tracey, many thanks to Greg and Zander, my special star, for your help and understanding in keeping all the balls in the air!

Peter, Tom, Tracey

Publisher's acknowledgments

We are grateful to the following for permission to reproduce copyright material:

Carlsberg A/S for use of the example of one of Carlsberg's must-win battles described in Chapter 5 and the example of Carlsberg's communications approach around the must-win battle journey described in Chapter 8; Professor Dan Denison for use of Figure 2.8, descriptions of the Denison Organizational Culture Survey in Chapter 2 and Appendix to Chapter 2; Roger Whittle for use of the Unilever in Africa boxed example from the IMD *Must-Win Battles Perspective for Managers*, No. 106, January 2004; Michael W. Garrett, Executive Vice President Nestle S.A., for analysis of critical issues faced by Joe Mueller during his early days as Market Head; C.J. van der Graaf, for Chapter 8, From tent to tent: the Unilever Ice Cream journey.

In some instances we may have been unable to trace the owners of copyright material, and we would appreciate any information that would enable us to do so.

The MWB journey

"Must-win battle" is a phrase that creates energy. The word "battle" suggests that there are competitors to be fought and defeated, and "must-win" implies the battles are urgent and important. So it is not surprising that senior managers who are unhappy with the current performance of their business find the idea of MWBs intuitively appealing, and it is not difficult to convince them that they ought to take their top teams away for a week to identify their MWBs and figure out how to win them.

And that is where we started, five years ago.

Since then, we have learned a lot. About how to choose the battles and how to win them. That reaching consensus and building commitment at the opening offsite event is, indeed, just the beginning of the journey. The bigger challenge is to mobilize the broader organization behind the chosen battles on an ongoing basis. An MWB can require a year or more of sustained effort, as is amply demonstrated in the Unilever Ice Cream journey recounted by its leader, Kees van der Graaf, in Chapter 8. As Kees makes clear, the journey does not get easier as it progresses – at no time can the leader sit back and relax, assuming that the journey will progress on autopilot.

The second thing that we have learned is that the must-win battle (MWB) journey should not be just an intellectual journey – figuring out what to do – it must also be an emotional journey. To win your MWBs you need people at all organizational levels to make an emotional commitment to the chosen battles and to begin to truly work together as members of a single team with shared objectives. The walls of the organizational silos have to be breached – permanently. This will take a shift in mind set, and that will not happen through a solely intellectual journey.

Our final learning is about leadership. We have worked with more than two dozen senior managers leading MWB journeys. Some are CEOs of major corporations, some are divisional managers within very large organizations, some are heads of medium-sized or smaller companies. Whatever their background and position, most find the MWB process becomes a personal leadership journey, as they discover that they cannot rely solely on the power of their position to force the organization forward. The same applies to their leadership teams. The focus has to shift to listening, assessing, persuading, and varying one's management style as the situation changes. As we will discuss in Chapter 3, "emotional intelligence" helps, but it is usually not sufficient. Sometimes the leader needs to take an unpopular position – disappointing key people – and courage becomes the order of the day. But these are not just isolated acts of bravery, the leader needs stamina, the courage to keep on asking the right questions, to keep pushing the organization toward the chosen goals when energy may be flagging.

As you will see, these three learnings underpin our approach to designing and leading MWB journeys. While none of the elements is new, combining them has proved very useful for leaders who want to cut through an array of uncoordinated initiatives, and bring focus and renewed energy to their organizations.

A brief aside: the limits of the military metaphor

Before we start it is worth saying a couple of words about the term "must-win battles" and its implied association with military strategy. Clearly, business and war are very different, both in their origins and their outcomes, and it would be disingenuous to compare the importance of adding to shareholder value with matters of life and death.

However, frequently the military metaphor is applied in business and there are significant lessons business can, and often does, learn about strategy and organizational leadership from military thinking. Military and business are both concerned with leading groups of people against purposeful and everchanging opponents, with one engagement not being an endpoint in and of itself but rather leading to yet another period of engagement. Both also recognize the importance of harnessing the intellect and the emotional commitment of their people toward a common external goal. But that is where the metaphor ends.

This book is intended for business organizations, led by leadership teams that are focused on winning in the markets in which they compete. It is about prioritization and choice. It is about intellect and emotion. It is about harnessing the power of the collective organization. It is also about, at each stage in the journey, taking stock and refocusing on the challenges ahead.

While winning each individual MWB is vital, the longer-term victory is to transform the organization into a cohesive team that can win these battles again and again.

We have written this book to provide a road map for managers who are sure the MWB approach is just what they need and who want advice on how to lead such a journey. But we have also written it for managers who are less sure of the approach but want to understand more fully what demands it would make on them and their organizations before they make a decision as to whether or not to proceed. So let's begin.

What are must-win battles?

The name says it all. MWBs are the 3–5 key battles that your organization absolutely must win in order to achieve its key objectives. That is a pretty short list. And while we find that most teams readily agree that focus is a good thing, they invariably find it difficult to agree on such a shortlist. Someone's priorities will not make the final cut. But avoid the trap of creating a long list of MWBs, because you will need to concentrate all your resources, and all management's attention, on your chosen MWBs. If the list is too long, both resources and attention will be dissipated, and you will end up with inadequate support for every battle. So be disciplined and be tough.

A well-chosen MWB has five characteristics.

An MWB should:

1. **Make a real difference.** The major criterion for determining what is
    and is not an MWB is impact. The key question is: "If we win this
    battle, what difference will it make?" The answer has to be that it
    will make a huge difference – not just to one part of the organization,
    but to the achievement of the company's overall objectives.

    This means, of course, that before you get serious about defining
    MWBs, your team needs to agree on what its overall objectives are.
    Most companies have a "mission" or "vision" statement, and these
    may be useful, but often they are too broad to provide the basis for
    developing MWBs. So what you need to identify before selecting
    MWBs are objectives that the management team really feel
    passionate about, along with the quantitative targets they need to
    meet to keep corporate office and/or shareholders on board.

    When Unilever in Africa embarked on its MWB journey, the first
    thing it created was a new vision statement that generated a lot of
    excitement: "We will touch the lives of all Africans by better
    anticipating and fulfilling their cleaning, caring, and nutritional
    needs, everyday, everywhere." "Everyday" was a key word, as it
    meant that products had to be low priced, in small packages, and
    distributed widely so they could be purchased on a daily basis.
    "Everywhere" meant that the parts of Africa where the company was
    doing less well, such as West Africa, would receive renewed
    attention. The vision was backed up by an ambitious target: "To
    double the sales in Africa in five years from €1.8 billion to €3.6
    billion and deliver above Unilever average value creation."[1] With
    this agreed vision and targets in place the management team created
    five MWBs, presented in the box below.

2. **Be market-focused.** Managers are often tempted to create MWBs that
    emphasize winning internal battles. Don't do it. Internal battles too
    often reflect the passion of executives who are competing among
    themselves for resources and attention. The point is to win in the

---

[1] See *http://www.unilever.com/Images/2002%20Africa%20Regional%20Group%20 20presentation_tcm13-5214.pdf* for further information on each of the MWBs chosen.
[2] Malnight, Thomas W., Killing, J. Peter, and Keys, Tracey S. (2004) "Must-win Battles," *IMD Perspectives for Managers*, Issue No. 106, March.

Unilever in Africa: must-win battles[2]

Unilever's African Regional Group has a long history of success, which has resulted in leadership positions in most of its major product categories. Underlying this success was a deep knowledge of local markets, a high-quality local talent base, extensive distribution networks, and a consistent flow of innovations. But in 2001 regional management recognized that many of its sources of success could be imitated by competitors and that future success would require a new focus that would create new energy. To achieve this it developed five MWBs:

- Everywhere (ensure Unilever brands are available everywhere in Africa).
- Everyone, Everyday for Life (providing for the everyday needs of all Africans).
- Priority Pillars for Growth (focusing resources around three key product categories critical for future growth).
- Winning West Africa (build West Africa to be as big as South Africa).
- Simply the Best (ensuring the strongest employees and operating culture working to the highest standards within the company, and with its communities).

The first MWB required a concerted effort to enter currently unserved geographic markets. The second meant that the group would build an additional €1 billion business in low-priced "popular products." The third involved focusing regional resources on product categories with the greatest long-term potential, even if they did not reflect corporate priorities in other markets. The fourth MWB involved balancing the regional geographic portfolio, moving away from a dependence on South Africa. Finally, the last MWB involved creating ways of working that would ensure the group could actually win the other four MWBs. Each MWB included specific measurable targets, and a specific set of actions required to win the battle.

Winning the MWBs would require managers who had been focused on delivering results within their territory to cooperate more broadly across the region. Some executives would become more dependent on others to meet their local objectives, losing much-valued independence. However, everyone realized that the collective opportunity could not be reached if each country continued to operate alone. And the commitment to a new way of working was made.

marketplace, not get a new transfer price from a sister division. Unilever Africa's management team created five MWBs, and one of those was an internal battle. That proportion is about right.

Specific targets underpinned each of these five battles, and sub-battles were identified that had to be won to support each of the main battles. We will say more about the creation of supporting battles in Chapter 7.

3. **Create excitement.** Your MWBs should be exciting – real challenges create real energy. Needless to say, you do not want your people charging off on hopeless quests that are impossible to win, but for maximum impact an MWB should focus on a collective objective that might previously have been thought impossible, such as dethroning a long-standing market leader. If your MWBs are not seen as exciting or meaningful by a large number of people in your organization, it will be difficult to maintain the commitment and resource trade-offs required to win them.

Some of your MWBs may be defensive – winning these battles will avoid calamities. Others will be more offensive in nature – moving into new markets, developing new technologies, taking market share from a larger rival, and so on. Both types of battles can be motivating, and in most organizations the final set of MWBs is a mixture of offensive and defensive challenges. There is no "rule" about this, the proportion of each will depend entirely on the circumstances in which the company finds itself. The Nestlé China example described below illustrates a situation in which defensive and offensive MWBs were under way at the same time. Both battles were won.

Nestlé China: don't kill the cows

When Joe Mueller took over as head of Nestlé China in 1998, the business was not performing well. Financial results were poor, and the organization was demoralized. As Joe put it: "Non-achievement of targets had become a habit." Part of the problem was that the company was processing far more milk than it could sell, and inventories of milk powder and condensed milk were bulging. One solution being discussed when Joe arrived was to tell farmers that Nestlé would no longer take the milk that their cows produced. The result, in all probability, would have been farmers with no means of livelihood, and slaughtered cows. One of Joe's first MWBs was to find a way to keep those cows alive! A classic defensive MWB.

At the same time Joe wanted to make an offensive move in the local market that would get a "win" for the company, and provide a much-needed employee morale boost. Joe's decision, implemented in record time, was to create a "Chinese Kit Kat" chocolate bar designed exclusively for the Chinese market. The new bar, both smaller and lower priced than the Kit Kats sold in Europe, was exactly what was needed for local tastes and budgets.

Both MWBs were a success and Nestlé China was turning in a strong financial performance within 18 months of Joe's arrival.

4. **Be specific and tangible.** MWBs need to be tangible and specific enough to be measured. MWBs that say "we must innovate more!" or "get closer to customers!" or "reduce costs!" are not useful. Your MWBs need to be specific to your business situation, markets, and organization. If you find it difficult to create specific targets and actions required to win your battles, chances are your MWBs are not sufficiently specific or tangible.

   Part of making MWBs tangible is to give them a reasonably short time frame. We usually find that more than half of the portfolio have a "time to victory" of two years or less. If the timeframes are too long, the MWBs may not generate much energy, and may be constantly displaced by other things that appear to be more urgent. Kees van der Graaf felt that two years was about right for some of his ice-cream business MWBs (see Chapter 8). But to Joe Mueller in Nestlé China, two years would have seemed much too long. He needed a quick win to boost morale, and he needed immediate action to get milk products flowing out of Nestlé warehouses so that farmers could continue supplying Nestlé with milk on a daily basis. Clearly, both company and industry conditions should have a major impact on the time to victory for your MWBs.

5. **Be winnable.** There is often a fine line between creating MWBs that are exciting – both aspirational and inspirational – and just plain impossible. An underperforming European beverage company

recently brought in a new CEO whose first job was to convince his best people – who were full of energy and ambition – that their first task was not to overtake the industry leaders but simply to start making promises to stock market analysts that the company could actually meet. In other words, one of their first MWBs was to regain credibility with the financial markets after a stream of broken earnings promises. Later, they would focus on becoming number one in the business.

One reason that management teams sometimes do choose MWBs that prove to be unwinnable is that they assume the competition will not react to what they are doing. The logic is more or less "we will take this action and then that action to win our MWB, and the competition will be so surprised (or asleep) that they will just stand by and watch us do it." Needless to say this is not what usually happens, and one of the exercises that we describe in Chapter 4 is designed to force the management team to get into the hearts and minds of stakeholders and competitors to prevent this "frozen competitors" assumption, which can easily lure the top team into unwinnable battles.

What problem are we solving?

If MWBs are the solution, what's the problem? Why do senior managers embark on MWB journeys? Although every manager we have worked with had his or her own reasons for the journey, what they had in common was a frustration with the current performance of their business and an impatience for improvement. They did not feel that incremental nudging or fine-tuning would bring about the necessary performance improvement. So they wanted to do something outside the norm to bring focus and energy to their teams, as their comments below indicate.

We had so-called priorities like "innovate more" which meant almost nothing. It was more a slogan than anything else. We needed to create real ownership of a few key priorities, that would bring us the passion, focus, risk taking, and entrepreneurship that we needed. Business as usual would not get us there.

We were too academic; we tried to make things perfect instead of making decisions. We were great at debates. Analysis drove out action.

We were a group of individuals in silos, not a team. There was no openness and even less trust. I had to break the prevailing mind set.

We were too internally focused, always talking about what we could and could not do. We need to concentrate on what we need to do to win in our markets and get on with it.

We were a group of talented people, producing mediocre results. The potential to do much, much better was there.

A careful reading of these quotes suggests that these managers actually faced two problems, in addition to the fundamental fact that their businesses were not performing well. One was that their organizations were not clear on where they were going because of too many initiatives or conflicting priorities, and the other was that their management "teams" were far from being teams. So one problem was a lack of shared strategic priorities, and the other had to do with the attitudes and behavior of the members of the management team. If this is the situation you face, your MWB journey needs to deal with both of these issues – it is no use focusing on one and ignoring the other.

For the reader who is not part of a large organization (and maybe does not want to be!)

If you are part of the leadership team of a small or medium-sized business you may feel that the issues facing the large international organizations that we discuss in this book have little in common with the challenges that you are facing. Our advice: do not stop reading. We have undertaken MWB journeys with companies like yours, and the issues are usually more similar than you might think.

First, Phase One of the MWB journey focuses on engaging a small team. Whether it is the top team of the company or the whole company staff, the same principles apply: you want to create strategic focus and get everyone committed to the new agenda. And even if you do not need the Phase Two cascade of the battles through the organization, you still need to embed the battles, create and maintain momentum around them, and monitor their success over time. Doing this in a large organization will be more complex than in a small one, but the challenges are similar.

Second, the marriage of intellectual rigor with emotional commitment is universally important. The leaders in the smallest entrepreneurial ventures probably know better than those in multinational behemoths that people with passion for a goal are critical for success. Just look at eBay, Google, or even BMW – all started small but had these vital characteristics.

▶

So, before you switch off, skim the rest of this chapter, if not the whole book, because we think, regardless of the size of your organization, you will find ideas and tools that can help you move your organization forward.

What is an MWB journey?

An MWB journey is an ongoing process, during which two things are happening simultaneously. One is that the team is learning to behave as a team, with shared objectives and a common agenda. The other is that MWBs are being identified, fought, and hopefully won. But because new battles will emerge over time, and corporate objectives may change, this part of the journey will never end; there will always be another battle to win. And although your managers may indeed become a team, as executives come and go the team will always be at least partially in flux, and will need continued attention to reinforce the shared agenda and expected behaviors.

Before you embark on your journey, you need to make an assessment of the starting conditions facing your business. We will discuss these shortly, but the key point is that not all MWB journeys are the same, and you need to tailor your trip to the particular conditions that you face in your business.

Phase One entails running a kick-off event for your team. This typically brings together the most senior managers in the company for up to a week in an offsite location to identify, through intense discussion and debate, the company's MWBs. The event ends with the selection of the MWBs and the senior managers who will lead them, and each member of the top team publicly committing to support all of the chosen MWBs. This first phase of the journey tends to be short and intense.

Phase Two involves the motivation and mobilization of the broader organization to win the chosen MWBs. For any given MWB this phase might last as long as several years, during which the organization must take ownership of each MWB, assemble and mobilize the resources to fight it, and win. But each MWB will follow a different course – some will move quickly and achieve early victory, others may lose their way and need to be re-energized or redirected. This phase demands stamina and persistence on the part of the company's leaders, as it is very easy for the organization to lose focus on the MWBs as the evolving pressures of day-to-day business throw up potential new priorities. And people who do not support the MWBs will do their best to slow things down and derail MWB activities. Such intransigents need to be identified and dealt with.

each phase of the MWB journey involves two sub-journeys, one emotional and one intellectual

Each phase of the MWB journey involves two sub-journeys, one emotional and one intellectual. The intellectual journey is necessary to ensure first that you select the right MWBs, and then that you choose the right supporting battles that need to be won to ensure victory in the main battles. The emotional journey should lead first to a new level of openness that will underpin the creation of a top management team that truly functions as a team, and then to a series of focused teams committed to winning each of the MWBs. Depending on where you are starting from, you may find one of these sub-journeys longer and more difficult than the other, and the exact balance between the sub-journeys needs to be tailored to your particular needs. One size does not fit all when it comes to designing MWB journeys.

We believe strongly that these sub-journeys need to run simultaneously. Some leaders are inclined to say, "Let's do the team building first and then we'll get to choosing the battles later," while others want to do the reverse. Our experience is that these approaches do not work well. Team building that does not focus on real issues does not take you very far, and MWB choices that have no emotional commitment to the result are a waste of time as they result in decisions that are never whole-heartedly implemented. And as the boxed commentary suggests, there is growing evidence that emotions and reason cannot be readily separated.

Emotions and reason are inseparable

We recommend that your MWB journey place as much emphasis on generating emotional energy and commitment as on intellectual rigor. Why? Surely executives, in fact *any* business person, should be as rational as possible and make decisions based on reason, i.e. intellectual weighing of the pros and cons?

▶

While we like to think this is what really happens – and have "programmed" executives for decades to try to put those niggling emotions aside – it's not. Huge advances in neurological sciences in the last decade or two suggest that emotions and reason are inseparable.[3] The processes by which we think, experience situations and respond to the dynamics in our environment are governed by a mix of emotional and rational responses. When we build experiences that we can apply to future situations, whether climbing a mountain or managing a change process in an organization, those embedded memories have emotions intertwined with "hard" facts. Think about how you responded when one of your team questioned an important aspect of the deal that you thought you had all agreed on, in front of the CEO of the prospective joint venture partner. Chances are, you had to control your anger and surprise before you could respond sensibly to this suggested change in plan (even if it was a good one). How much will you trust that person ("this turncoat") in future?

Such experiences leave "markers" in your brain that can act as short cuts in future situations when you see similar patterns. Despite millennia of evolution, we still have the fight or flight instinct when we feel under threat – emotions are driving. Apply a similar concept to business experiences and you get "gut feel." Gut feel is increasingly recognized as an important component of leadership. Because the situations leaders face are complex and often ambiguous, requiring the management of people and relationships as well as big-picture vision and planning, they rely on instinct to help them create short cuts through the complexity. Many leaders are very good at recognizing patterns which activate, often unconsciously, experiences they have had before. These help them make choices faster and more surely than they might otherwise have done.

But – and it's a big but – using these short cuts can block as well as promote courses of action. Say the person who had embarrassed you at the meeting came to you with a new suggestion. How thoroughly would

---

[3] If you would like to read more on this topic, the following are books that we have found useful, though obviously there are many, many more to choose from:
- Antonio Damasio's work including (1) *Descartes' Error* (1994), Picador; (2) *The Feeling of What Happens: Body and Emotion in the Making of Consciousness* (1999), Harcourt Publishers Ltd.
- Howard Gardner (2004) *Changing Minds The Art and Science of Changing Our Own and Other People's Minds* Harvard Business School Press, USA.

you consider it? If your relationship had not improved, odds are that you would not look at it in as positive a light as if someone you trusted had made the suggestion. The point is that the brain's short cuts include your emotions as well as your rational side. Unless you recognize these dynamics it can be difficult to be open to new perspectives and opportunities.

And it's not just being open with yourself about your emotions. Another key learning from psychology and neuroscience is that everyone has their own view of the world. Our information gathering is selective and biased by our own interpretations of events, which is based on our experiences, values, and beliefs, all of which have emotional and rational dimensions. We each see the world differently – and this impacts the way we do business. So it is important to be open with the people around you, about emotions as well as intellectual ideas, and about how these impact your view of the world. Unless you understand how your world view colors your interpretations it can be hard to find common ground with others.

Business people need to stop acting as if they can subjugate emotion to reason. Without recognizing and managing the impact of emotions, decision making and action will be impaired because we don't always challenge our short cuts as we should, or appreciate that others see the world very differently.

The key is to recognize emotions as an equal partner of intellectual rigor and idea generation. If we succeed in doing this, the ability to foster strong relationships between people and to leverage the experience of the group and organization will not only improve decisions but also drive shared commitment to action. The MWB process is one way to recognize this interplay of emotion and reason – and get it into the open where it can be managed to greatest effect. Because you probably have the same marker in your head as we do: people make or break a strategy.

We now consider each phase of the journey in more detail.

Phase One: engaging the team

No two MWB journeys are exactly the same, nor should they be. Every business starts the journey from a different place and, as mentioned earlier, every executive who is to lead an MWB journey should begin by making a careful assessment of the "starting conditions" facing his or her business before designing the journey.

Assessing starting conditions

Starting conditions will impact on your choice of the MWBs, the urgency surrounding their execution, and the relative emphasis to be placed on the emotional side of the journey versus the intellectual side. You simply cannot plan for an optimum journey if you have not first had a close look at your starting conditions.

Every business sets out on its MWB journey from a different starting place. Some are in great financial health. Others are in crisis. Some have a management team that truly is a team, in others the team is in complete disarray. Some have a clear sense of the future, others have scarcely thought about it. And so on. These differences can mean, for example, that one organization could have a significant emotional challenge ahead of it to get everyone working toward the same objectives, while for others, who work well together but don't make good strategic choices, the challenge will be more on the intellectual side.

Before embarking on an MWB journey we suggest that the leader assesses the four starting conditions identified in Chapter 2. These will impact both the design of the kick-off event and the subsequent activities required to engage the rest of the organization. We have found, for instance, that some organizations are eager to implement the MWBs chosen at the kick-off event, while others will greet the new imperatives with dismay and comments like: "Here we go again, another flavor of the month – I wonder how long this one will last." The final starting condition, discussed in Chapter 3, is the readiness of the leader to lead the journey. It is a demanding challenge, and not everyone is ready for it, even if it is what the organization needs.

With the starting conditions identified, the leader can design the kick-off event, paying particular attention to who will attend, the topics to be discussed, and its duration. In our experience the kick-off event can involve anywhere from ten to forty managers, and on occasion may consist of two shorter events rather than one longer one. However, we believe the offsite should include at least two and preferably three or four overnight stays, and should be held in an unusual location. You want people to get "away from the office" both mentally and physically.

Mapping Phase One of the journey

The kick-off event should center on the three clusters of activity identified in Figure 1.1: "open windows," "define and agree battles," and "commit to one agenda." Your first reaction on looking at this figure may be, "why all the fuss?" Why not simply start with defining and agreeing on the battles? Surely that has to be the first step, and then in Phase Two, you engage the organization to win the chosen battles. Well, yes and no. In fact, no.

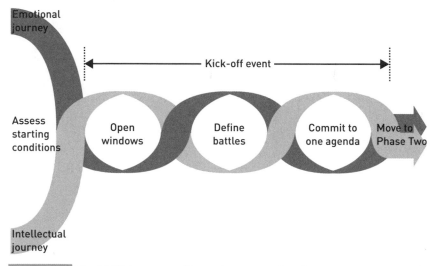

Figure 1.1 The MWB journey – Phase One: engaging the team

The problem is that while you may think that defining a shortlist of MWBs would be an intellectual process – why this battle is more vital to the future of our organization than that one – it is also very much an emotional process involving personal aspirations and fears, such as, "will my projects and concerns make it onto the final list?" Because the chosen MWBs will receive the lion's share of the firm's resources and management attention for the coming months and years, other things will have to be cut back or eliminated. All of this means, of course, that creating a shortlist of MWBs is going to result in winners and losers among the management team members. So choosing MWBs is definitely an emotion-laden process.

The question is whether these emotions will come "on to the table" during the discussion or will be hidden, emerging much later to subvert the implementation process. To avoid this possibility, you want an open and honest debate when you are choosing your MWBs. But a full-blown MWB debate is a difficult context in which to start personal discussions, which is why we recommend that you engage in "opening windows" – especially emotional windows – before you move to debate the MWBs.

Opening windows

Opening windows exercises are, in effect, "warm-up" events to start the group moving gently forward on both the intellectual and emotional journeys in parallel. In Chapter 4 we describe seven exercises that we have used to "open windows" with a number of teams. The aims are to build a shared understanding of the challenges and opportunities facing the business, and at the same time have people discuss their personal feelings about how the team works together, and their role in it. The exercises range from personal ones such as asking each participant to describe their lifeline, to "outside-in perspectives" during which participants get into the "hearts and minds" of shareholders, customers, competitors, or perhaps regulators.

The more personal exercises will start the group on the emotional side of the MWB journey, while the others build the intellectual side. Whether you choose to spend more time opening emotional windows or on intellectual exercises will depend on your starting conditions. The farther you judge you have to go on the emotional side, the more emphasis you will put on opening the personal windows, and vice versa.

Defining and agreeing MWBs: colliding to decide

Of course you cannot open windows forever, you need to get to the heart of the matter, which is deciding on the MWBs. The best way to begin is to review the criteria outlined earlier in this chapter, and then create a long list of potential battles. This gets everyone thinking about what is a MWB and what is not. As you begin to shorten the list some battles may be repositioned as sub-battles of others. Others will be thrown out on the grounds of not having enough impact, not being winnable, and so on.

It will take several iterations to complete the list, and we recommend these discussions do not all take place on the same day – a night for reflection, talk at the bar, and a good night's sleep are necessary parts of the process. When the list is finished, you need to review it to see whether all the battles taken together are winnable. Each on its own might be feasible, but as a group they may be too much. You cannot undertake them all with the resources you have. At that point the conversation often turns to timing issues – could we sequence the battles in such a way as to make the whole list feasible? This also leads to the question of which of the current activities we need to stop doing in order to free up the resources needed for our MWBs (the "must-stops").

Defining and agreeing on your MWBs is likely to produce some real stress points on your MWB journey. Suddenly this process, which may have been regarded by some of your executives as a relatively harmless waste of time, is getting real. Everyone wants their pet projects or their part of the business to feature on the final list of MWBs. That is not going to happen.

As we discuss in Chapters 3 and 5, this is a testing time for the leader. The key is making sure you get the real issues on the table during the debates, and deciding how long to let the debates run. The leader who arrives at the kick-off event with a fixed idea of the right list of MWBs and imposes his or her will is in trouble. There will be no buy-in and the battles are unlikely to be won. On the other hand, as we point out later, selecting MWBs is neither a democratic process nor a popularity contest. If the MWBs are chosen on the basis of who is supporting them rather than intellectual rigor, you have a problem.

In addition, the losers – for there will be managers who perceive themselves as losers in this process – have to be kept on board, because you will need everyone to do their part in ensuring that the chosen battles are won, even those who did not support all items on the list as it was being created.

Committing to one agenda

The final stage of the kick-off event, "committing to one agenda," is one of the most important parts of the emotional side of the MWB journey. It is a vital step in the process of building a real team at the top of the organization. Not only are the most senior managers in the company committing to give their full support to all of the chosen MWBs, whether they are directly involved in them or not (or initially supported them or not), they are also committing to working together as a team at the top. Shared goals and shared accountability will be the order of the day from this point forward. Silo walls are coming down, for good. This new attitude is perhaps best captured by the manager who explained: "If I win the MWB that I am leading by using all of the resources you need to win yours, that is not a win."

Leaders who want to get the members of their team to commit to the chosen MWBs and begin to adopt new supportive behaviors usually use a combination of "carrot" and "stick" approaches. The carrot is, "look at the great and successful future we can build together – which is so much better than our situation today." The stick is, "if you do not support these MWBs and adopt this new behavior there will be no place for you in the organization," We do not believe that fear is a successful long-term motivator, and you do not want to begin your journey with everyone feeling that they have been coerced into joining the trip. So the more you can use the carrot approach the better.

If you are a new leader, you will learn a lot about your senior people during the kick-off event. You may learn that some are not willing to come on the MWB journey with you. Especially on the final day, when people are committing to new ways of working together, you are likely to be challenged by key players who do not want change. They may even have formed a coalition to stop the MWB journey before it gets started and decided to push you to the limit. "Do you really intend to go through with this?" will be the question, in one form or another. Your answer, demonstrated in both words and deeds, has to be yes.

Of course, creating an emotionally charged day during which managers pledge to work together and behave differently to support one another in the future is only a beginning. The real test is in what happens in subsequent weeks and months. But it is an important beginning, and the end of the first phase of the MWB journey. So what should you have achieved by the end of Phase One? These are the outcomes that we believe you should shoot for in your kick-off event:

1. **Shared understanding of the challenges and options facing the organization.** Opening windows is critical to get everyone on the same page in terms of understanding the full picture of the challenges that are facing the organization and the options for addressing them. In particular, this part of the process has to promote openness between the team members that allows them to appreciate the different perspectives that others may bring, as well as laying the foundation for improving teamwork and cooperation across traditional organizational barriers or boundaries.

2. **An agreed list of 3–5 MWBs.** These are the critical battles that the organization needs to win in the next year or two to move toward its desired vision of the future, both in terms of business performance and how the organization works together.

3. **A committed team for each MWB.** During the second half of the kick-off event the leader will assign the team leaders responsible for each MWB. Others may be added to each team when the group returns to the office.

4. **A high-level action plan for each MWB.** High-level action plans will be created for each MWB during the kick-off event. More detail and depth will be added to the plans once the group returns to the office and expanded teams are created.

5. **New ways of working together.** The whole group will leave the kick-off event having committed to new ways of working together. This group agenda is broader than any individual MWB, and should lead to a permanent change in behavior.

6. **Individual commitments.** Each individual at the kick-off event will commit to personal actions and behaviors necessary to win the MWBs and to support the new group behavior. This means not only supporting colleagues but also holding each other accountable for achieving targets.

7. **An initial assessment of the starting conditions for engaging the organization.** Before returning home after the kick-off event, the team need to think through how members of the organization will react to the MWB agenda and how best to engage them. And, of course, what needs to be done immediately on return to the office.

Phase Two: engaging the organization

As you return to the office with your team, you must communicate to the broader organization the decisions that you have made, why you have made them, and the team's commitment to the new agenda. For greatest impact the team should appear personally in front of an audience of key people and explain what they went through – both intellectually and emotionally – during the kick-off event. Pull no punches. Explain the debates and why the group came out where it did on the key issues. Make it clear that the team saw the week as a turning point for them as individuals and as a group. And as a turning point for the organization. Leave no one in any doubt that things are going to be different.

The danger in returning to work (back to the "swamp" as we call it in Chapter 7) is that the team will be sucked inexorably back into the day-to-day activities that they have been away from for a week, and within three weeks it will seem as if the kick-off event never happened. Difficult as it is, it is the job of the leader – and the team – to prevent this.

In Chapter 7 we discuss in detail the stages of the engagement process highlighted in Figure 1.2. As with the kick-off event, this process requires addressing both intellectual and emotional journeys. Intellectually the challenge is to demonstrate to the entire company that the MWBs make sense. Given the situation the business faces, these are the key challenges, and their selection was driven by reason, not politics.

emotionally the challenge is to motivate people to commit to their part of the journey

Emotionally the challenge is to motivate people to commit to their part of the journey, even though this is likely to mean working across silos in ways they have never done before. You need to create energy and forward momentum throughout the organization. Without winning both the intellectual and emotional journeys, the whole effort will become

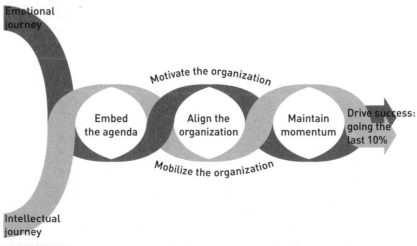

Figure 1.2 The MWB journey – Phase Two: engaging the organization

just another initiative that went nowhere, and the question "So what's different after this offsite?" will be perfectly valid.

Embedding the agenda

In the weeks following the kick-off event you need to start the process of embedding the MWB agenda at the "heart" of the organization, to make it the central focus that will guide all future priorities and actions. The first step is to establish communication of the type we previously described: personal, open, face-to-face, and consistent. It's not a one-off "this is what we did on our offsite" exercise; you need to put in place channels for ongoing communications, which you will use again and again after the first waves of excitement about MWBs start to ebb. (They will.) Lou Gerstner, Chairman and CEO of IBM from 1993 to 2002, and current Chairman of the Carlyle Group, says so, and so do we.[4]

Then the leader of each MWB needs to start bringing on board the people who will become important members of the MWB teams but were not at the kick-off event. These teams are very likely to have a cross-silo composition. Their first task is to create more detailed versions of the action plans sketched out at the kick-off. The early plans will not be perfect, but you need them now because until you have a first cut on the who, what, when, where and how, the MWBs cannot start to move forward. Because the teams will often bring together people who may not know each other, it is important that as they develop the detailed plans, they use many of the same exercises as the team at the kick-off event. Opening windows, debating the critical actions and discussing team and individual roles and behaviors will build the shared understanding of the actions, resources, and capabilities required to win, and the commitment to the new ways of working that will underpin delivery of their action plan.

Your plans are an important first step, but you are also going to need the core processes of the organization, meaning the planning, budgeting, monitoring and reward systems, to support the new direction. Often these systems are difficult to alter but you need to do it because if you do not the old systems – which support the old behavior – will prevent progress. It will take more than a couple of weeks to

[4] Gerstner, Louis V., Jr. (2002) *Who Says Elephants Can't Dance: Inside IBM's Historic Turnaround*, HarperCollins Publishers, London.

make these changes, but get started now – because changing how performance is monitored and how people are paid, just to pick two examples, will tell the broader organization that you are serious about the new agenda. And make sure that reviewing MWB progress is front and center at all leadership team meetings. If the MWBs are to become the priority for the organization, they must be the continual focus of the team.

The final, and probably most difficult, part of embedding the MWBs is making available the time and resources for whole-hearted action. You cannot simply add the MWB agenda on top of ongoing activities – the result will be widespread burnout and cynicism. At the offsite you and your team decided what the organization would have to stop doing to free up the time, resources, and energy to win the MWBs. Now you have to make those "must-stops" a reality. This will be a challenge, as some of them are likely to be fiercely resisted. To win the battle of the must-stops, you will need an aligned organization.

Aligning the organization

No company can win its MWBs through the efforts of the leadership team alone. The broader organization has to buy into the new agenda. How you create this buy-in will very much depend on how ready various parts of the organization are to embrace the MWBs. When they learn of them, are people going to say, "Thank goodness, at last we are moving forward," or "They must be kidding, that is not possible."? Getting the organization aligned behind the MWB agenda has to be planned carefully – both in terms of where to start and how fast to move. But again, don't delay, because building a broad organizational commitment to winning the battles is going to take time, so the sooner you get started the better.

Getting the organization on board and ready for action requires several steps. First the team as a whole has to make very visible its commitment to the new agenda, as discussed previously. The MWB agenda must then be cascaded through the different organizational units of the company, through mini-versions of the kick-off event, because their active buy-in and support are critical to delivering the MWB agenda. The original MWBs are not up for debate, but the supporting battles, which need to be won to bring victory in the overall battles, need to be identified, agreed, and implemented. Then you need to repeat the cascade events down into the organization as necessary, with senior managers running the events, making the link to previous events, and removing roadblocks when needed.

The final component of getting the organization aligned is to bring on board those much-maligned (depending on which side of the fence you sit) staff people at headquarters. Generally the corporate center does not have external markets, so it is not likely to have MWBs of its own. However, the expertise of the central staff can be very important in helping the various MWB teams. So use the staff groups, do not isolate them. If they feel left out, they may hamper the journey.

Maintaining momentum

As the MWB cascade continues you will need to actively encourage and support the new management behavior that everyone committed to at the kick-off event, as well as keep track of how well the MWBs are delivering against their milestones and targets.

We suggest that you start reviewing MWB progress on a regular basis, beginning about six months after the kick-off event. Monitor both movement toward "hard" targets such as revenues, new markets entered, or products launched, and softer behavioral issues. The latter are very important because managers who are resisting the new ways of working can destroy the atmosphere that you want to create. Do not allow the reviews to become endless debates. Make decisions, and ensure that there is wide recognition for exceptional performance and visible consequences for under-performance.

If your early reviews show that your team is coming together, energy levels are high, and the MWB battles are well defined and starting to be fought, you can give yourself a pat on the back. At this point, your journey is truly under way. But – and there is always a but – there will inevitably be hiccups along the way. Some battles may get derailed, others will just never really get going. It is important to recognize (early, hopefully, because the battles are constantly on the team agenda) when things are off track. Often you will need to re-energize the battle, perhaps by making some personnel changes. But sometimes you will need to refocus the battle or abandon it. In a changing world, fixed strategic priorities are seldom a recipe for success. So the last big challenge is to know when to declare victory and replace an existing MWB with a new one. After a significant investment of emotional energy and resources, parting with an "old friend" may be difficult, but do it. The next challenge is waiting for you.

Getting an organization moving in a new direction, and keeping it moving, can be exhausting. Some teams have compared the early months of an MWB journey to trying to get a heavy flywheel moving. They put in lots of energy, but there is little visible movement. To build momentum, you and your team will continually need to support each other to sustain your collective commitment and your ability to keep generating energy in others. Clearly, positive early results help, so be sure to celebrate these and broadcast them extensively. But also create opportunities which will allow the team to maintain and reinforce the emotional relationships they have built. If the team lose spirit, you do not have much hope of moving the rest of the organization forward.

In Chapter 7, we suggest that the final determinant of success is "going the last 10 percent" – doing the small things that are hard to describe because they are so varied, from sending a handwritten thank-you note, to throwing a party, to just showing up when you are not expected. These seemingly small acts can make a huge difference to the mind set of the organization and become the stuff of enduring organizational legend.

Creating a sustainable competitive advantage

Most MWBs focus on market-related initiatives: developing and introducing new products, reviving a brand, entering a distant geographic market, or a new segment in a home market, and so on. By definition these battles are important. But competitors will respond to your moves – doing their best to copy or exceed your efforts, and acting in ways that will take away the uniqueness of your offering to customers. It is very difficult, in short, to create a *sustainable* competitive advantage. A better market objective in today's world is often to create a *renewable* competitive advantage.

But we believe that you can use your MWB journey to create a real sustainable competitive advantage. This is the creation of a management team that truly functions as a team. As we have argued, and will again in Chapter 3, top managers rarely function as teams. So if you can build your key players into a real team, you will have a competitive advantage that will be very difficult for competitors to match. Your top team, operating as a team, should be able to implement new initiatives more quickly and with more force than competitors. In other words, having a sustainable competitive advantage in the way people work together at the top of your organization should allow you to create a series of renewable competitive advantages in the marketplace.

As the leader your most important job is to take that group of people at the top and turn them into a team. It will not be done overnight, and it may not be possible with the cast of characters that you have in place right now. The MWB journey is a tool we have seen managers use to build such a team, but let us re-emphasize that the key is to simultaneously lead your people on a journey that is both intellectual and emotional. This is difficult because it means that the leader has to continuously embody the blend of both intellectual and emotional openness that he or she is asking of others. The rewards, however, in terms of business results as well as the personal development of the leader and of the team members, are great.

If you are attracted by the possibility of using an MWB journey to create focus, energy, and a real team in your business, read on. We offer you a guide to the journey, including tools and techniques that can be used at each stage, plus advice on how to use them. These are not just nice ideas, we have personally used these tools, and seen MWB leaders use them. They work.

As you move forward through the book, you may wonder whether the MWB approach is right for your company – and for yourself as a leader. The questions below are, hopefully, useful prompts for your deliberations.

1. **Is an MWB journey what our business needs?**
   Assess the health of your business, management team, strategy and organization. If performance is good, the top team is functioning well and the organization is working effectively, you probably do not need an MWB journey. However, if this is not the case, you should consider the ideas and examples in the book and decide whether the journey would make sense for you.

2. **Could we move forward on simultaneous intellectual and emotional journeys?**
   The power of the MWB approach is in building commitment to action at the same time as defining strategic priorities. If you are comfortable with this idea, and your business needs to improve on both dimensions, then keep reading. If, however, you feel that separating strategic planning and team building is the best way forward, then MWBs are not the right solution for you.

3. **Are the most senior managers capable of handling such a major change?**
   Most top teams need to change their behavior and mind set in order to lead a successful MWB journey. This change process can be particularly difficult if your organization is made up of independent fiefdoms led by strong-willed managers. Building these executives into a team will require a lot of debate and conflict, and as the leader you will need to manage the process. In spite of the fact that some managers will see themselves as losers in these debates, you need to keep them on board because you need everyone participating in your team at the top.

4. **If we get started, will we be able to sustain the momentum?**
   After the kick-off event you will need to build a broad coalition of managers from all levels who will drive the MWB initiatives deep into the organization. How difficult will this be? How willingly will the organization at large embrace the idea of MWBs? You will have to monitor progress carefully, and find ways to re-energize the MWBs as you go.

5. **Given the challenges, are you ready to lead the journey?**
   Do you have the skills and deep desire to lead such a journey? You will have to demonstrate a lot of flexibility and be willing to enter debates with an open mind, not always insisting on getting your way. And this will be an ongoing journey. Do you have the stamina? Stopping part way through is worse than not starting.

If your answer is yes to most of these questions, you should give serious thought to undertaking an MWB journey. If not, we nonetheless hope that you will find food for thought in these pages, and recognize the power of combining clarity of strategic focus with emotional commitment. Because whatever field and situation you are in, whatever the size of your business, strategic clarity and personal commitment are critical to achieving your goals.

Now, meet Jan Ryan. He's a fictional character, but knows many of the senior managers we have worked with intimately because each of them is part of him.

Here is the roadmap for the journey he is about to embark upon.

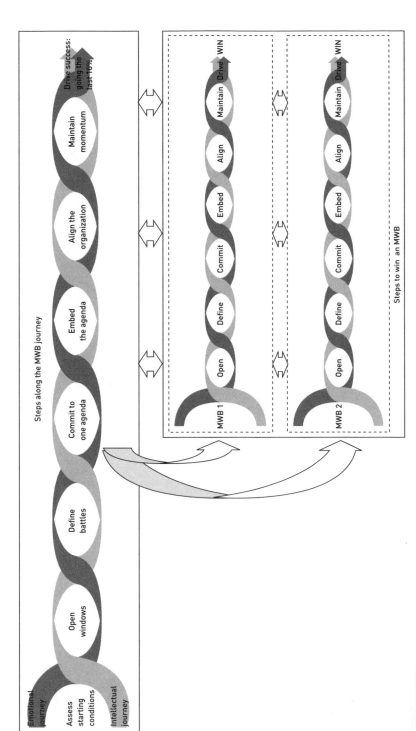

Figure 1.3 The MWB journey roadmap: an overview

Preparing the journey	Engaging the team		Making it happen: engaging the organization		

Intellectual journey

Assess starting conditions — Open windows — Define battles — Commit to one agenda — Embed the agenda — Align the organization — Maintain momentum

Drive success: going the last 10%

Emotional journey

1 Leader believes strongly that s/he wants to launch journey – and is prepared to lead it

2 Leader/team are clear about where the company is starting from, what key issues (business, team, organizational) need to be addressed by the journey

3 Kick-off event is planned (who, where, what, when, how)

4 Team builds a shared understanding of the challenges and opportunities facing the business

5 Team starts to discuss how they work together; the role of the individual, and issues surfaced

6 MWBs are debated, defined, redefined, and agreed

7 Leaders are chosen for each MWB and high-level action plans developed

8 Commitment is made by the team, and each individual within it, to new ways of working together to support winning of the MWBs; the MWBs and behaviors together define the MWB agenda

9 Commitment is made by the whole team to drive the MWB agenda

10 Key messages are developed to start to engage the organization

11 MWB agenda is embedded in the organization: communications, core processes, monitoring, time and resources, must-stops

12 Team make their commitment to the agenda visible throughout the organization, new behaviors are modeled continuously

13 For each MWB, detailed action plans and broader teams are defined; mini kick-off events ensure shared understanding of actions and commitment to new behaviors; action launched

14 MWBs are cascaded through the organization, with supporting battles defined

15 Corporate centre agenda (actions, new ways of working and behaviors) is defined to support MWB agenda

16 Progress against MWB targets and desired team behaviors is reviewed regularly, with consequences

17 Battles that are not meeting targets are refocussed, accelerated or stopped

18 Communications of successes and lessons from failures are ongoing

19 Battles are won, new battles are defined to replace them

20 Leadership teams go the last 10%

Figure 1.4 Steps along the MWB journey

Preparing the battle

Engaging the MWB team

Making it happen: engaging the organization

Emotional journey

Assess starting conditions

Intellectual journey

Open windows

Define battles

Commit to one agenda

Embed the agenda

Align the organization

Maintain momentum

Drive success: going the last 10%

1 MWB team leader is committed to and excited by his/her battle

2 Initial small MWB team develops detailed action plans, broader team and resource/capability requirements

3 Broader team meets at mini kick-off event to develop shared understanding around the battle

4 MWB team agrees key actions required to win the battle; sub-teams and sub-battles needed across the organization

5 MWB team commits to drive the battle forward

6 Responsibilities are assigned to drive key activities

7 Commitment is made by all team members to new ways of working together and behaviors that will be required to win the MWB

8 Key messages are developed to start to engage the organization around this MWB

9 MWB activities and targets are built into communications, core processes, monitoring, time and resources

10 The MWB activities and sub-battles (if needed) are cascaded to all organizational areas involved, with mini kick-off events as required for supporting battle teams

11 MWB team leader is active in all broader MWB agenda cascade events, as appropriate

12 Progress against the specific MWB targets and desired team behaviors is discussed regularly with management, with consequences and corrective action as required

13 Communications of successes and lessons from failures are ongoing

14 The MWB team goes the last 10%

15 Victory is declared

Figure 1.5 Steps to win an MWB

Preparing the journey

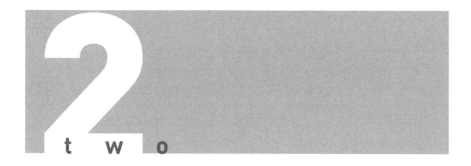

two

Understanding your starting conditions

Jan Ryan raised his head and scanned the table. Nine managers, with nine different opinions – again. After three hours of debate there was still no progress. Everyone was polite, but frustration was not far below the surface. Since taking over as CEO of the Europe division two months earlier, Jan had been tempted to let several managers go, but part of him recognized a deeper truth: "We have a leadership problem: and I am the leader."

Jan had spent his first months in his new role assessing the business and the management team he had inherited. His suspicions were that the persistent decline in business performance was going to worsen, and he did not believe that the managers were addressing the key issues. They knew the future did not look good but no one was really focusing on it – they were all preoccupied with trying to meet their current performance targets.

On the few occasions that Jan had persuaded his managers to think about the future, everyone seemed to have a different opinion – and these seemed to be based as much on gut reaction as on in-depth analysis. Even more worrying was that no one in the leadership group was sharing their thoughts with the others – each was doing his or her own thing. The result was a huge number of uncoordinated initiatives producing few positive results.

In fact, Jan had discovered more than twenty ongoing initiatives. Six were called "strategic thrusts," and had titles such as "reconnecting with the customer" and "refocusing the brand portfolio." Another aimed to embed a "single-minded passion for winning" across the organization, and two others focused on creativity. On the growth front, one project involved building a growth vision, while yet another, separately, focused on building commitment for growth. External consultants were also looking at future growth opportunities. In addition to these Europe-wide initiatives, Jan found a whole range of projects at the country level – again with little coordination between them.

When Jan met with each member of his team individually to get a better understanding of the challenges facing the division, it became clear that they shared his frustration. One manager summed it up:

> We have initiative fatigue – too many priorities means no priorities. We do not need more new ideas. We need to integrate and act on what we already know. We talk too much and do too little.

But there were clearly cultural hurdles to be overcome if this were to happen:

> We have a blame culture. No one takes risks because there are no rewards for getting it right, there is only blame for getting it wrong. The country heads seem to have an unspoken agreement – you don't ask any tough questions about my operation and I won't ask any about yours. They are very nice to each other.

After listening to these comments Jan concluded that something needed to be done to break the cycle of stagnation and decline, or the group would soon have a crisis on its hands.

Your four starting conditions

The sentiments that Jan heard in his first two months as CEO are familiar to many executives. Everyone is frustrated, but no one seems able to move forward. As the frustration mounts the leader concludes that something out of the ordinary must be done to break the paralysis. Jan was tempted to take his team offsite for a week to begin to "sort things out," but he realized he would need some sort of framework to shape the event or it would just be a week of aimless debate, going in circles. So he was interested when his human resources manager gave him a description of the MWB concept, and was particularly drawn to the idea of MWBs as a two-phase process, which first involved the senior management team, and later the whole organization.

Jan commented:

> I realized immediately that a two-stage journey made sense. First a week offsite with the senior management group to select the MWBs and begin to build them into a team, and then after we come back to the office, we would begin the process of motivating and mobilizing the rest of the organization to win those battles.
>
> The thing that caught my attention immediately was the list of four starting conditions (see box) because I realized that what I had unconsciously been doing in my first months as CEO was, in effect, to try to determine what those starting conditions were for us.
>
> I had definite opinions about where we were in terms of (1) the current and expected performance of the business, (2) the health of the management team, and (3) the appropriateness of our current strategic priorities, but I did not know if the senior managers agreed with me. And I was not at all sure about number 4, the overall health of our organization.

Starting conditions

1. **Current and expected operating performance of the business**
   What is the current performance and outlook for the business?
   Excellent? OK? Poor? Close to crisis? In crisis?

2. **Health of the management team**
   Do the managers function as a team?
   Do they have shared goals, and shared accountability for results?
   Are the right people on the team?

3. **Appropriateness of current strategic priorities**
   Does the management team have the right strategic priorities,
   given the issues that the business is facing?

4. **Overall health of the organization**
   How healthy is the organization, beyond the level of the management team? Will it be ready to engage in the chosen MWBs?

In this chapter we will discuss each of the four starting conditions in turn, and conclude by indicating how the design of your MWB journey should reflect your starting conditions.

Starting Condition One: current and expected operating performance

Before setting out to determine their MWBs, Jan and his team needed to develop a shared sense of how well the business was performing currently, and how well it was likely to perform in the near future. This fundamental performance assessment underlies many of the debates that take place during a kick-off event, impacts the group's choice of MWBs, and heavily influences the pace and urgency of the whole MWB journey.

A new leader like Jan needs to have an independent view of the performance of the business, over and above what he is told by his managers. To develop such a view we recommend a close look at financial statements and analysts' reports as well as visits to major customers, competitors, suppliers, and perhaps regulators. Such visits will give a feel for the way the company is perceived externally and may flag intangible issues that the numbers do not reveal. For example, if customers or suppliers are reluctant to meet you or seem to be guarded when you speak with them, there may be issues you need to probe.

In addition, and especially if you are a new leader, you should supplement this data review with one-on-one interviews with the management team. This is where you will start to understand the "real," often unspoken issues. For example, Jan heard that implementation was a problem – too much talk, too little action. The challenge with such interviews is to make sure you get honest feedback. If you sense that you are not getting sufficient open and honest feedback from your group it may be helpful to use an impartial third party to conduct interviews with your team.

As we have said, Jan suspected that the business he had inherited was not healthy. But he recognized that his managers were closer to the markets than he was, so he concluded that before they embarked on the MWB journey they should meet as a group for an intense and thorough discussion about the performance of the business.

To drive such a conversation we frequently use the performance curve, shown in Figure 2.1. The curve portrays the changing performance of a business over time. Initially the business is doing well, increasingly well, and then performance gradually flattens out and begins to decline. The decline is gentle at first, and then picks up speed and the business

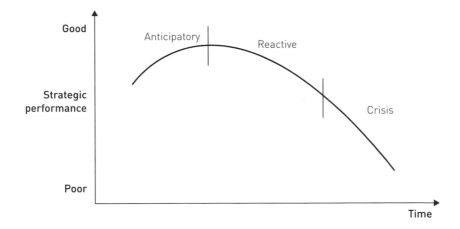

Figure 2.1 The performance curve

Source: Crossan, Mary M., Fry, Joseph N., and Killing, J. Peter (2005) *Strategic Analysis & Action*, Sixth Edition, Prentice Hall, Toronto, Canada.

ends up in crisis. (We must emphasize that sliding down this curve is not inevitable, if management acts in time.) The question for a management team is: where are we on this curve?

If you are in the anticipatory portion of the curve, for example, current performance will be good and the immediate outlook also good. However, you may nevertheless see signs that change will be required and the challenge is to act before business performance starts to decline. At the anticipatory stage of the curve, your MWBs will focus more on the longer term and building the capabilities you need to keep winning in the future.

If your business is in crisis, it is usually easy to convince your team that something needs to be done. Your MWBs will have a short-term orientation and will probably be financially driven. However, even in crisis we would advocate that some of your MWBs have a longer-term focus, as once the crisis is over the company will still need the capabilities to compete successfully. Cutting all research and development (R&D) may help you survive the next six months, for example, but rebuilding your R&D department after the crisis may take years. And competing with no new products may not be possible. So while taking a longer view can be difficult, because your executives will be in fire-fighting mode and want to fix only the immediate problems, you have to do it, otherwise the actions you take to get through the crisis may kill you later. An MWB journey that starts in a crisis situation needs to include a longer-term view, even though everyone's emotional energy will be focused on the short term.

Jan believed that his business was in neither crisis nor the anticipatory portion of the curve, but was rather in the middle of the reactive area. Performance was clearly declining but the business was not yet in crisis. However, he found, as do many leaders, that his people did not all agree with him, or with each other. Some thought they were at the top of the curve, at the end of the anticipatory stage, whereas others thought they were in the reactive stage – but the estimates ranged from "early reactive," through "mid-reactive" to "late reactive." No one thought they were in crisis. There were, however, a great variety of opinions about how long it would be before they were in crisis if they did nothing.

Jan was delighted with the wide-ranging debate as his managers became less polite with each other and discussed issues ranging from "what do we mean by strategic performance?" to "is our performance decline temporary or likely to continue?" It was agreed, finally, that they were probably in the mid-reactive area of the curve. That positioning persuaded many of the group that, as suggested in the box below, this meant they needed to get started on their MWB journey immediately, and that the journey needed to result in early action – not just more debate.

Prevailing conditions and management issues on the change curve

	Anticipatory	Reactive	Crisis
Prevailing conditions			
Strategic performance	Healthy	Sliding	Critical
Need for change	Uncertain	Becoming clearer	Clear
Time pressure	Have time for experimentation	Have to get change started	Urgent – start now, Move fast
Internal commitment for change	Low	Mixed	High
Management capability	High	Mixed	Low

	Anticipatory	Reactive	Crisis
Management issues			
Strategic	Is change really necessary?	How permanent is the decline? Where to start the change?	Achieving rapid pace of change.
Organizational	Lack of willingness to try anything new. Today's performance is fine.	Dealing with resistors who think the status quo is fine.	Who to rely on? How good is the leader?
Personal	Credibility of leader who thinks change is required.	Power to move the resistors aside.	Links to past. Job security.

Source: Adapted from Crossan, Mary M., Fry, Joseph N., and Killing, J. Peter (2005) *Strategic Analysis & Action*, Sixth Edition, Prentice Hall, Toronto, Canada.

Starting Condition Two: health of the management team

Most top management "teams" are not, in fact, teams. This argument was made by J. R. Katzenbach[1] in his classic article "The Myth of the Top Management Team." Katzenbach argues that the "natural overachievers" (his phrase) who typically make it to the top of the organization are used to acting as individuals with clear accountability and a clear area of responsibility. They have little inclination to be part of a team at the top if that means committing to a shared purpose and shared accountability for mutually held goals. In fact many groups at the top do not even try to work together effectively. The top "team" is actually a series of one-on-one relationships as each senior manager interacts solely with the CEO.

We have found that there are three types of top management groups: (1) the truly dysfunctional, (2) the average collection of hard-working managers not functioning as a team, and (3) the true high-performing team. A quick summary of each type is provided in the box.

[1] Katzenbach, J. R. (1997) "The Myth of the Top Management Team," *Harvard Business Review*, Nov–Dec.

Management "teams"

Dysfunctional	Average	High-performing
The group is rife with jealousies and engages in destructive interpersonal competition. Animosity is rife. The leader has little authority.	Managers are out to further their own position, but not necessarily at the expense of others. Each focuses on his or her part of the business and relationship with the CEO. There are few shared goals.	The group is in fact a healthy team, with shared goals and accountability, meeting the criteria in the box on p. 41.

In a truly dysfunctional group, managers actively try to bring about each other's downfall while simultaneously promoting their own position. These groups are so dominated by personal rivalries and antagonism that the business issues never get discussed in a rational way. The question becomes not "is this a good idea?" but rather "whose idea is this?" and if the wrong person is sponsoring the idea, it will never be agreed. One classic example of a dysfunctional management team was the group at the top of AOL Time Warner after its ill-fated merger. Interpersonal battles were rampant, as managers from one predecessor company routinely tried to upstage those from the other in internal meetings and in front of clients. The end result was a business disaster, and many of the senior managers were ultimately fired.[2]

An average management group is not nearly so destructive as the AOL Time Warner group, but managers do tend to act as a collection of individuals, not as a team. Each executive typically has a decent working relationship with the CEO, but relationships with others around the top table are not particularly cooperative. In some groups, like Jan's, conflict is avoided: everyone is polite so that others will be polite in return. "I do not ask any questions about your part of the business and you do not ask any questions about mine." If the leader is new to the group, as was Jan, he may not yet be accepted as the leader.

The characteristics of the high-performing team are presented in the box below. In our experience such teams are rare, but we have seen

[2] Klein, Alec (2003) *Stealing Time: Steve Case, Jerry Levin, and the Collapse of AOL Time Warner*, Simon & Schuster, New York, USA.

"average" management teams make substantial progress toward the ideal state depicted in the box over the course of an MWB journey.

The high-performing management team

- The team accepts the leader.
- The team communicates honestly and openly.
- Each individual is committed to the team agenda, and his or her personal agenda supports the team agenda.
- The managers respect each other.
- The team handles conflict effectively.
- Once a decision is made, everyone supports it.
- The team has legitimacy in the eyes of others.
- Team members feel mutually accountable for results.

Do you have the right managers for the MWB journey?

A successful MWB journey can take an average management group a long way toward becoming a high-performing team. But such a journey is unlikely to change a truly dysfunctional group into a high-performing team, or for that matter change individual dysfunctional managers into team players. In our experience, it is impossible to have a successful MWB journey with a dysfunctional management team. So before you set out on an MWB journey you need to give serious thought as to whether or not you have the right people in your management group.

If you have read Jim Collins's best-selling book *Good to Great*,[3] you will recognize this advice, as Collins also argues that you need to get the right people "on the bus" before you set out on your journey. Only after you have the right people on board, and in the right seats, Collins asserts, is it the time to make adjustments to your strategy.

The same advice applies to MWB journeys. The members of your management team will be tested many times during the journey: by you, by their peers, and by their subordinates. After the kick-off event the team will be watched closely for any evidence to suggest that the new priorities are not real. Subordinates will ask: "Will we really give

[3] Collins, Jim (2001) *Good to Great*, Random House Business Books, London.

up some of our autonomy to another part of the organization? Why should we stop one of our favorite projects?" And so on. The new mind set, which says that the MWBs will get first priority in decision making and resource allocation, will be a real struggle for some managers.

Of course, making changes in the team is more easily said than done, especially for the CEO who has been in the job for some time and has avoided making the changes she knows she should have because of past loyalties, debts owed, and battles fought. The weight of history often leads to inaction. But this is where the MWB process truly starts – getting the right team in place. Sometimes we see management changes made before the kick-off event, but just as often the changes take place after the event as during that offsite week the leader gets a much better feel for the members of the team, and personnel decisions which may have been avoided are now seen as essential.

the members of your top management team will be tested many times during the journey

We were recently discussing the MWB concept with a CEO who told us of his multi-year struggle to get the right team in place. His story began when he was recruited to take over a troubled public company in the late 1990s. He described his first encounter with his new management team:

> After I had been in the company about six weeks and traveled around the US and Europe meeting everyone and getting a sense of the issues that we faced, I decided that we needed to get the top team together to discuss the situation and hammer out some priorities. I asked everyone to set aside a day and a half for the session.
>
> We duly met, and to my complete surprise, we seemed to be finished after two and a half hours. I did an initial presentation outlining what I had seen during the six weeks, and what I thought we needed to do. There was no debate. Everyone just said OK.
>
> I was amazed. I had worked for twenty years in a successful global company that debated things in depth, and at sessions like this everyone was determined to show how smart they were and that they had something to add. Although painful at times, the process was on balance a good one, and I felt that this was what management should be.

Although I had run large divisions in my old company, this was the first time I had ever been at the very top – CEO of a public company – so I was not sure what to expect. Could it really be this easy? I was pretty certain of my own judgment – but did I really hit a complete bull's-eye in that opening presentation? It seemed like maybe I did. We broke up, and everyone returned to their individual operations to implement my ideas.

After six months, it was clear. Nothing had happened. These managers were so used to being told what to do that unless I went to every operation and provided a continual stream of instructions, they were incapable of making progress. My conclusion was that I had the wrong people.

Over the next few years this CEO replaced about seventy of his top one hundred managers, hiring what he described as "dogs with teeth," by which he meant managers who could think for themselves and would fight for their ideas. The key MWBs facing the company were local, and many of the new managers successfully cleaned up their parts of this far-flung company. However, in 2002, when the CEO concluded that it was time to pull the organization together and create "one company" with a set of common global brands and a common face to suppliers and customers, many of the managers rebelled and continued to fight for the independence of their unit. The CEO tried for "far too long" (his words) to turn them into team players, but in the end he gave up and replaced four or five key people. In doing so he realized another truth: "It is far harder to fire people that you have hired yourself than those who were put in place by your predecessor." New MWBs, he reluctantly concluded, required a renewed management team.

This CEO's situation was perhaps extreme, but it dramatically illustrates the cost of having the wrong team in place as you set out on your MWB journey.

Starting Condition Three: appropriate current strategic priorities

Some management groups really have their act together in terms of strategy. In the words of former Chairman and CEO of General Electric, Jack Welch, they "see the world as it is, not as they wish it were." They know where they want to get to, and are well on the way to getting there. There is no way to be sure, but after twenty years of working with senior managers, we suspect that such teams are in the minority. In the following box we have documented two other approaches to setting strategic priorities that we frequently encounter: those that operate more on the basis of personality than data, and those that are drowning in data but do not seem to know what to do with it.

Approaches to strategic priorities

Priorities based on personalities, not analysis	Drowning in data but no clear, shared priorities	Appropriate shared strategic priorities
1. Opinions and gut feel replace business analysis. No real, recent market data.	1. Books of data, but no real meaning given to it.	1. Shared and realistic understanding of business performance and organizational health.
2. Performance measured against budgets, not external measures.	2. No shared sense of the desired future.	2. Shared view of the desired future.
3. Strongest personalities win strategic arguments.	3. Many differing views on the best way forward.	3. Shared agreement on the major issues facing the business.
		4. Battles that need to be won have been clearly identified.

As Jan reviewed the four points in the right-hand column of the box, his earlier opinion that his management group was a long way from having appropriate strategic priorities was confirmed. During his one-on-one interviews with his managers, he had probed four key strategic areas, to see how wide the divergence of opinion really was. The next box illustrates the types of questions he was attempting to answer and gives a sample of the answers he received. He found the overall pattern of responses discouraging, and alarming.

Testing for shared strategic priorities

Key areas and questions	Sample responses from Jan's management team
Overall goals for the business: ● Do we have similar goals for the business? ● Are there shared aims, for example in terms of growth targets, profitability, and risk?	*Manager A:* We must grow our European revenues, so our American parent will give us more attention, respect, and resources. *Manager B:* We must keep our people employed. We cannot become one of these "hire and fire" companies. *Manager C:* We must increase our profitability – overall size is not the issue.
Product/market priorities: ● Does the management group agree which products and markets are key for the future? ● Which should get the priority when it comes to the allocation of scarce resources, such as money to build brands, and development time?	*Manager A:* We mus create European versions of our parent's newer products to reduce our dependence on our aging, core product line. *Manager B:* Creating new products, based on our existing European technology, is vital to renewing our growth in our core markets. *Manager C:* Taking our existing products beyond today's core markets to the countries that have just joined the European Union must be the key to our future growth.
Value to customers: ● Is there agreement on how we should compete in our markets? ● Do we know why customers will prefer our offerings to those of competitors?	*Manager A:* We must compete on innovation, not price. *Manager B:* Developing European brands, not just national brands, will lead us to greatly increased market share. *Manager C:* If we can get our quality consistently right, we will win. ▶

Key areas and questions	Sample responses from Jan's management team
Outsourcing: ● Do we agree which activities the business will perform itself and which will be outsourced?	*Manager A:* We should outsource as much as possible to give ourselves flexibility. We do not, for example, need to own our delivery trucks. *Manager B:* To quickly enter new markets in Eastern Europe we will need to use joint ventures, but to regain control we should buy out our partners as quickly as possible. *Manager C:* To increase quality levels we need as much control as possible – and that means doing things ourselves. Outsourcing our IT to India, for example, would be a disaster.

A review of the responses in this box reinforced Jan's view that identifying and focusing on a limited set of MWBs was vital for the business. He knew there would be strong resistance to settling on "only" four or five battles. But he was convinced that selecting more than five battles would make no sense. If they did that, everyone would just continue as they were. And he knew already that he was going to have to push the group very hard to identify the things they would stop doing. The MWBs could not just be added to a list of ongoing initiatives that was already too long.

Starting Condition Four: overall health of the organization

Since he had taken over as CEO, Jan's focus had been on the management team, and by his own admission he could not "see" very far into the organization. He did not know many of the people reporting to his direct reports, for example, and he knew very few managers in mid-level positions in the country organizations. Certainly no one was giving him informal feedback on the organization's processes, structure, culture, or even the level of morale in various parts of the organization. He did not have a real feel for "how we do things around here."

To see what he could learn, Jan decided to take the advice of his human resources manager and run a "Denison organizational culture survey,"[4] which could be used to poll (anonymously) as many people as he wanted in the organization and get their responses to sixty questions about how the organization worked. It was the nature of the questions (see page 53) that convinced Jan to run the survey. He commented:

I really liked some of the survey questions. My assumption was that we would score poorly on everything related to strategic intention, goals, and vision. At least that's how I would have scored us, but I really did not know what the broad population of managers thought. I hoped they would score us low because that would mean they were seeing the same reality that I was.

On the other hand I thought that we would probably do well on customer focus – as we do service our existing customers well – we just do not spend any time thinking about people who should be our customers but are not. With respect to working in teams, I would say that we operate as teams within the organizational silos, maybe, but between silos the score should be poor. Co-operation between different parts of the business – that should be a zero!

I hope the survey will have credibility even with our skeptics, because it has been used with more than 1000 companies over a fifteen-year period, and our results will be compared with theirs.

Jan decided to run the Denison survey with the top 350 people in the organization, and 310 of them completed the questionnaire. The results are shown in Figure 2.2. Jan was not surprised with the outcome, but some of his managers were both surprised and upset. He explained:

We had a meeting to discuss the Denison results. In retrospect it was funny, although it did not seem so at the time. Some of the managers were demanding to know "who filled in this survey" as if they wanted to punish the respondents! Then, when they realized that we had more than 300 responses, they retreated a bit and realized the results had to be taken seriously. The next wave of defensiveness was when each claimed that the poor responses must have been coming from other parts of the organization. And so on.

[4] For more information on the Denison Organizational Culture Survey, copyright © by Daniel R. Denison, developed by Professor Denison of IMD, please see *www.denisonculture.com*.

Finally everyone calmed down, and we agreed that we had a lot of work to do in setting strategic priorities. They seemed to feel (but did not quite have the nerve to say) that the low teamwork, and coordination and integration scores just meant that there was no cooperation between countries – which was fine with them.

I would say that by the end of the discussion most people, but not all, were ready to admit that a week offsite might not be a complete waste of time. The question that I needed to work on was what we would actually do during the week.

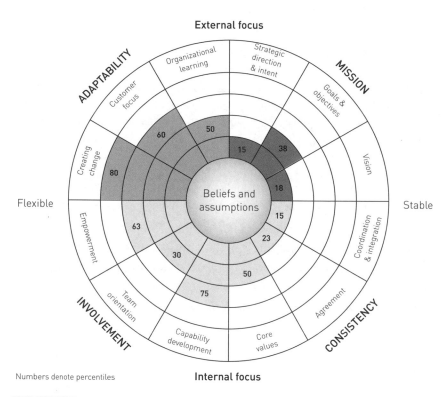

Numbers denote percentiles

Figure 2.2 Denison survey results

How to read a Denison culture survey
Definitions

The four quadrants of the survey focus on:

● Involvement: building human capability, ownership, and responsibility. *Ask:* "Are our people aligned and engaged?"
● Consistency: defining the values and systems that are the basis of a strong culture. *Ask:* "Does our system create leverage?"
● Adaptability: translating the demands of the business environment into action. *Ask:* "Are we listening to the marketplace?"
● Mission: defining a meaningful long-term direction for the organization. *Ask:* "Do we know where we are going?"

The survey questions are included on pages 53–8.

Interpretations

The most important point is: the more shaded areas in the survey result the better. More shading on an element means it is stronger, as measured by the percentile figures. The percentiles compare your organization's scores on each element against the average scores of other organizations that have taken the survey. For example, if an organization is placed in the 80th percentile, like Jan's on creating change, this means it is stronger on this dimension than 80 percent of the companies in the database (over 500 companies at present). Conversely, scoring in the 15th percentile on strategic direction and intent highlights a significant problem in Jan's case (not a surprise!).

Few companies are uniformly strong in all aspects of their culture, so understanding your organization's health in each area is useful for thinking about strengths that can be built upon and weaknesses that need to be countered as you develop your MWBs. Strength (or weakness) in combinations of the different quadrants is correlated with higher (or lower) performance in relevant aspects of the business:

● Mission and Consistency scores (indicating level of stability) tend to impact financial performance measures such as return on assets (RoA), return on investment (RoI), and return on sales (RoS).

● Consistency and Involvement (internal focus) tend to impact quality, employee satisfaction, and return on investment. ▶

● Involvement and Adaptability (flexibility) typically impact product development and innovation capabilities.

● Adaptability and Mission (external focus) generally impact revenue, sales growth, and market share.

Denison's research, over more than a decade, suggests that the most effective organizations, i.e. those that perform well, have a balance in strength across all the quadrants. They are likely to have cultures that are adaptive, yet highly consistent and predictable, and that foster high involvement, but do so within the context of a shared sense of mission. For more information, please see *www.denisonculture.com*.

Mapping the journey

Jan was aware that an MWB journey could last as long as two years, and felt that it was impossible to plan the trip in detail at the outset. ("It is like climbing a mountain or raising a child," he said. "You plan as much as you can, but you have to respond to events as they occur, so the overall journey is something that evolves over time.") He felt the same philosophy should apply to the one-week kick-off event, but nevertheless was very concerned about where the emphasis should be placed during the week. As he discussed the possibilities with his human resources manager he drew the diagram in Figure 2.3, highlighting the two starting conditions that concerned him most: the extent to which the managers truly functioned as a team, and the extent to which they had appropriate strategic priorities.

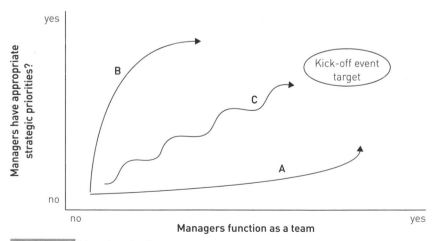

Figure 2.3 Mapping the journey

Jan explained his thinking as he drew the diagram:

> There is no doubt in my mind that we are somewhere near the bottom left corner of this chart, although I realize that not everyone on the management team would agree. I must say in their defense that the top group is not actually personally destructive toward each other – this is not AOL Time Warner after the merger. But we are not anywhere near being a true team. And I know for certain that we do not have appropriate strategic priorities. In fact, I would agree with the manager who said that we have so many priorities that we have no priorities. The Denison results reinforce this. So the question is not so much where we are starting from as how we get from where we are to the top right corner.

As Jan drew the starting conditions diagram on a whiteboard, his human resources manager readily agreed that they were somewhere near the bottom left corner, and argued that what they needed to do first was build the managers into a more effective team. He thought a week together away from the office doing trust-building exercises should be the next step. This would be the emotional journey – route A on Jan's diagram. However, Jan was not so sure. He knew that the vice president of strategy thought that the managers worked together "well enough" and the first thing they needed to do was get the vision and strategy clear and then they could work on the "team stuff," as he called it. In other words, start with the intellectual journey – route B. Jan himself was wary of either approach and thought that it made more sense to try route C and "go up the middle" – which meant the kick-off event would be a journey that combined both intellectual and emotional components. He explained:

> I have been on team-building events before. They have an impact, but because there are no real business decisions being made, I find it all rather artificial. We can work together to build a bridge across the river faster or more creatively than the other teams of managers, but that does not mean that when we get back to work, I am going to agree with your five choices of must-win battles.

> On the other hand, we really do need people to open up emotionally, otherwise there will be no genuine commitment to the battles we choose, and nothing will happen. So if we can do it, the agenda for the week has to be both intellectual and emotional: we need an honest and open intellectual debate about must-win battles that ends up with real emotional commitment to the outcome.

Like Jan, our experience suggests that for best results your MWB process needs to draw on both the intellect and the emotions of your management team. If you underplay the intellectual – meaning that you are not rigorous and thorough enough in your analysis – you will probably choose the wrong MWBs. But if you underplay the emotional content – meaning that the team does not commit emotionally to the new way forward – your implementation will suffer.

your MWB process needs to draw on both the intellect and the emotions of your management team

Having said that, you should certainly adapt your kick-off event to suit your starting point. Think about the strengths and weaknesses of your group as you put together a possible agenda. What aspect is normally most underplayed? Whatever it is, we would suggest you open with that to indicate that this event is going to be different. For example, if you normally focus on the intellectual side of strategy and analyze "strengths, weaknesses, opportunities, and threats,"[5] or perhaps use Porter's five forces analysis,[6] start instead with the *hopes and fears* exercise we discuss in Chapter 4 that gets people to begin to discuss emotional issues at the individual level.

However, if you never talk about the management team and how the team work together, use the *myths and taboos* and *how we resolve conflict* exercises which force attention to the dysfunctional side of the way in which the group operates. For example, you and your group will already have a characteristic decision-making style. It may tend toward "quick and dirty" at the expense of thoroughness, or it may be in-depth, detailed, and feature endless debates. In one company we have worked with the decision was seen as the "starting point for the debate," meaning that people argued with the decision for months after it was made, rather than implementing it. The *how we operate as a*

[5] Hill, T. and Westbrook, R. (1997) "SWOT Analysis: It's time for a product recall," *Long Range Planning*, vol 30, no 1. A critical assessment of the use of SWOT analysis.

[6] Porter, Michael E. (1980) *Competitive Strategy: Techniques for analyzing industries and competitors*, Free Press, USA. We do not discuss these analyses here as they are widely used and well covered elsewhere in the business literature.

team exercise put this approach in stark focus and laid the foundations for new ways of decision making. These exercises are described in Chapter 4.

By the end of the kick-off event you should have covered both intellectual and emotional topics. But bear in mind, too, that as the event unfolds, your planned activities may change in response to crises, team discussions, or decisions reached. As a result we suggest you do not begin your event by giving the group a detailed schedule of activities. That will make some people uncomfortable, but you need to maintain your flexibility. You have to be clear about your desired destination before the event begins, but the exact route will be determined as you go.

One more issue

After his human resources manager left the office, Jan took a deep breath and looked out of the window, blind to the traffic in the parking lot below. The MWB journey sounded attractive, and he was convinced that it was the right thing for the business. There was, however, one more issue – a big one – that he needed to consider before he committed himself and his team to beginning the journey: Was he capable of leading it?

The Denison survey: questions
(Copyright © by Daniel R. Denison)

Respondents to the survey questions below are asked to assess how strongly they agree with each of the following statements with reference to their own organization (on a scale of 1 to 5 where 1 is strongly disagree and 5 is strongly agree). After assessing their organization for each individual item (question), the respondents then develop an overall assessment for each index based on their answers to the five items for that index.

The questions for the four quadrants and the indices within each (definitions in italics) are as follows:

Involvement

Index	Item
Empowerment Individuals have the authority, initiative, and ability to manage their own work. This creates a sense of ownership and responsibility toward the organization.	1. Most employees are highly involved in their work. 2. Decisions are usually made at the level where the best information is available. 3. Information is widely shared so that everyone can get the information he or she needs when it's needed. 4. Everyone believes that he or she can have a positive impact. 5. Business planning is ongoing and involves everyone in the process to some degree.
Team orientation Value is placed on working cooperatively toward common goals to which all employees feel mutually accountable. The organization relies on team effort to get work done.	6. Cooperation across different parts of the organization is actively encouraged. 7. People work like they are part of a team. 8. Teamwork is used to get work done, rather than hierarchy. 9. Teams are our primary building blocks. 10. Work is organized so that each person can see the relationship between his or her job and the goals of the organization.
Capability development The organization continually invests in the development of employees' skills in order to stay competitive and meet ongoing business needs.	11. Authority is delegated so that people can act on their own. 12. The "bench strength" (capability of people) is constantly improving.

Index	Item
Capability development (cont.)	13. There is continuous investment in the skills of employees.
	14. The capabilities of people are viewed as an important source of competitive advantage.
	15. Problems often arise because we do not have the skills necessary to do the job. (Reverse Scale)

Consistency

Index	Item
Core values Members of the organization share a set of values which create a strong sense of identity and a clear set of expectations.	16. The leaders and managers "practice what they preach."
	17. There is a characteristic management style and a distinct set of management practices.
	18. There is a clear and consistent set of values that governs the way we do business.
	19. Ignoring core values will get you in trouble.
	20. There is an ethical code that guides our behavior and tells us right from wrong.
Agreement The organization is able to reach agreement on critical issues. This includes the underlying level of agreement and the ability to reconcile differences when they occur.	21. When disagreements occur, we work hard to achieve "win-win" solutions.
	22. There is a "strong" culture.
	23. It is easy to reach consensus, even on difficult issues.
	24. We often have trouble reaching agreement on key issues. (Reverse Scale)

▶

Index	Item
Agreement (cont.)	25. There is a clear agreement about the right way and the wrong way to do things.
Coordination and integration Different functions and units of the organization are able to work together well to achieve common goals. Organizational boundaries do not interfere with getting work done.	26. Our approach to doing business is very consistent and predictable. 27. People from different parts of the organization share a common perspective. 28. It is easy to coordinate projects across different parts of the organization. 29. Working with someone from another part of this organization is like working with someone from a different organization. (Reverse Scale) 30. There is good alignment of goals across levels.

Adaptability

Index	Item
Creating change The organization is able to create adaptive change. The organization is able to read the business environment, quickly react to current changes, and anticipate future changes.	31. The way things are done is very flexible and easy to change. 32. We respond well to competitors and other changes in the business environment. 33. New and improved ways to do work are continually adopted. 34. Attempts to create change usually meet with resistance. (Reverse Scale) 35. Different parts of the organization often cooperate to create change.

Index	Item
Customer focus The organization understands and reacts to the customer, and anticipates their future needs. It reflects the degree to which the organization is driven by a concern to satisfy the customer.	36. Customer comments and recommendations often lead to change. 37. Customer input directly influences our decisions. 38. All members have a deep understanding of customer wants and needs. 39. The interests of the customer often get ignored in our decisions. (Reverse Scale) 40. We encourage direct contact with customers by our people.
Organizational learning The organization receives, translates, and interprets signals from the environment into opportunities for encouraging innovation, gaining knowledge, and developing capabilities.	41. We view failure as an opportunity for learning and improvement. 42. Innovation and risk taking are encouraged and rewarded. 43. Lots of things "fall between the cracks." (Reverse Scale) 44. Learning is an important objective in our day-to-day work. 45. We make certain that the "right hand knows what the left hand is doing."

Mission

Index	Item
Strategic direction and intent The organization's plan is to "make their mark" in their industry. Clear strategic intentions convey the organization's purpose and make it clear how everyone can contribute.	46. There is a long-term purpose and direction. 47. Our strategy leads other organizations to change the way they compete in the industry.

▶

Index	Item
Strategic direction and intent (cont.)	48. There is a clear mission that gives meaning and direction to our work. 49. There is a clear strategy for the future. 50. Our strategic direction is unclear to me. (Reverse Scale)
Goals and objectives A clear set of goals and objectives can be linked to the mission, vision, and strategy, and provide everyone a clear direction in their work.	51. There is widespread agreement about goals. 52. Leaders set goals that are ambitious, but realistic. 53. The leadership has "gone on record" about the objectives we are trying to meet. 54. We continuously track our progress against our stated goals. 55. People understand what needs to be done for us to succeed in the long run.
Vision The organization has a shared view of a desired future state. It embodies core values and captures the hearts and minds of the organization, while providing guidance and direction.	56. We have a shared vision of what the organization will be like in the future. 57. Leaders have a long-term viewpoint. 58. Short-term thinking often compromises our long-term vision. (Reverse Scale) 59. Our vision creates excitement and motivation for our employees. 60. We are able to meet short-term demands without compromising our long-term vision.

three

What does it take to lead an MWB journey?

As he pondered launching his business on an MWB journey, Jan Ryan wondered if leading it would really be so different from his daily work as a CEO, or from the previous five years he had spent as the head of a large division of Strand, a global British company. He suspected that the issues he would face and the skills he would need to lead the MWB journey would not be new to him.

We disagreed. In our opinion MWB journeys present unique opportunities and challenges to the executives who lead them, and not every senior manager possesses the skills to be an effective journey leader. If you are new to the business, as Jan was, you will be interacting on a personal level with executives whom you do not know well, so you may find yourself in unexpected and perhaps quite emotional situations. While the early part of the journey will present an opportunity for you to learn more about your managers, equally, the whole of the team is going to learn a lot about you and see how you react to a variety of situations in an unusually intense setting. The bottom line is that for a newly installed manager, the early stages of an MWB journey present a clear opportunity to establish yourself as the leader, but the situation is likely to be very challenging. High risk with the potential of high reward.

However, a leader who has been in the business for some time is likely to be using the MWB process to upset the status quo, as most MWB journeys do not have as their objective the continuation of "business as usual." New energy and new focus are the order of the day. This means, in fact, that as an established senior executive you may have a more difficult time than a newcomer would have. First of all, you are saying that what was "good enough" yesterday is suddenly no longer good enough. You may have been tolerating "satisfactory under-performance" and now you will not. The rest of the group will be saying, "what's gotten into Harry?" Second, as the established leader you may have a difficult time in recognizing or acting on long-standing problems, as they may be the result of your own initiatives. As the CEO in the previous chapter said, it is always more difficult to see the flaws in people (or initiatives) you have chosen yourself.

In Figure 3.1 we summarize some of the challenges and opportunities facing new and established leaders as they embark on MWB journeys. Much depends, of course, on the performance of the business at the time the MWB journey begins.

The management team	**Functions well**	As the new leader you need to establish yourself. If the business is performing well, you can use the MWB kick-off event as a major learning opportunity. If it is not, you can use it to find out why not. In this case, your challenge may be to convince the team they have to change.	As the experienced leader you have created a management team that works well together. The MWB challenge will be to identify the major issues facing the business and build commitment to the way forward.
	Does not function well	As the new leader you may need to change the management team prior to the MWB process. But do you know enough? The MWB kick-off event may be your first in-depth look at the individuals and the way they work together.	As the experienced leader you may be part of the problem. You have allowed the unhealthy team to continue. You will need to find a way to make a sharp break with the past, and establish new ways of working together, while leaving yourself room to change too. The MWB kick-off event should be a good place to start.
		Yes	No

Is the leader new to the business?

Figure 3.1 Leadership challenges and opportunities

Leadership imperatives

Whether you have recently become the leader of the business, or have been in the job for some time, we believe that there are three things you will have to do successfully to lead your MWB journey. We call these "leadership imperatives" and believe they are different from the day-to-day challenges most managers face. As the leader:

1. You have to "own" the journey, from the preparation for the kick-off event, through the kick-off, and until the battles are finally won, modified, or abandoned, which could be as much as two years later.

2. You must insist that difficult choices be made, but you cannot make all of those choices yourself.

3. You have to find ways to build the management group into a team, and ensure their ongoing commitment to the MWBs.

In this chapter we examine each of these imperatives.

Imperative One: the leader must own the journey

An MWB journey is not a "quick fix." During the course of the journey there will be unexpected setbacks and in these testing times everyone will be looking to you, not just for answers but to see whether you still believe that the battle is the right one, and that the goal is worth fighting for. This is when you will be most severely tested. Persistence, belief in the end goals, and stamina matter. If you show any signs of doubt, the word will spread quickly. As one MWB leader said to us: "Celebrating success is the easy part!"

An MWB journey consists of two stages, and the leader has an important role to play in each. During the kick-off event you are the catalyst, the person who leads by example, persuades, insists, energizes others, listens intently, and still has energy when others are tired. You are realistic and at the same time optimistic. Realistic about what is possible. Optimistic that the process will bring major benefits for the business and the people in it. You are supportive of the process, even when you are not exactly sure where it is heading next. You do not rely solely on the power of your position, you persuade and motivate as necessary. Everyone is watching and you are being tested in a very public way. This is leadership at its most visible.

Given the challenges involved, many leaders use a facilitator to help plan and lead parts of the kick-off event. If you do this, be careful. As the leader you have to own the MWB journey – both intellectually and emotionally. No outsider, be it a consultant or facilitator, can be seen to be "running the show." Using a facilitator allows you to take a participant role from time to time, and take a break from leading the process, but you must ensure that you are the one driving the key decisions as the process unfolds. We discuss the pros and cons of using a facilitator on page 88.

Even while the kick-off event is in full flow, most leaders are thinking about what will happen after the event. They know that they cannot drive forward four or five MWBs on their own. They are going to need help. So the key is to identify the people who will comprise the leadership teams of each of the MWBs. Even though you must own the overall journey, these teams will own the individual battles, and they will create the energy needed to cascade the battles into the broader organization. These teams must expand and broaden as time goes on, creating sub-teams ever deeper in the organization.

The MWB teams will cut across the traditional functional, product, or geography-based organizational silos – that is one of the benefits of the MWB process – but you do not want them to become new silos in themselves. Your challenge is to ensure that as new sub-teams are built, each is linked to the team above it, and is horizontally in touch with the others. We suggest you choose team leaders who are by nature not very territorial, or make assignments that clearly give managers responsibilities well beyond their existing silos.

As time passes and the kick-off event becomes a distant memory, your primary job is to keep everyone focused on the MWBs and keep re-energizing the team so that they can energize their own MWB teams. In addition, it is your job to ensure that with accountability and responsibility is a heavy dose of consequence. Actions and results, not nice words, will be the key to winning the battles. Winning battles at the office requires commitment and ownership of the follow-up process, not just by the leader but by the team, and subsequently by their teams. Keeping everyone at the same table and moving forward over time is a significant leadership challenge. As the story of Unilever's Ice Cream business in Chapter 8 illustrates, carefully planned events to celebrate success can very effectively recharge everyone's batteries, as well as setting the stage for the next round of implementation. As we said in

Chapter 1, it helps a lot if your MWBs are inherently exciting. Inspirational and aspirational battles that everyone feels are winnable will help you keep the drive alive. Hope creates energy. Ownership creates commitment. Accountability, with consequence, creates action and results.

We mentioned in the opening paragraph that unexpected setbacks will test your resolve as your journey progresses. But so will new initiatives. In any healthy business, as the months pass, new and competing demands will arise for resources. Will the MWBs be forgotten or diluted? Your challenge is to find the right balance between staying true to the MWBs, and recognizing that the world does change – frozen priorities are seldom a recipe for success. Owning the journey does not mean becoming blind to anything that was not agreed at the kick-off event.

Two final notes. First, although fear can motivate people in the short run, our experience is that in the long run you are much better advised to create and sustain energy with positive reinforcement. Provide opportunities for people to build positive relationships – it helps immensely if people enjoy working together to win their shared battles. Secondly, part of owning the journey is removing the people who are consistently blocking progress. They slow down the process, if not derail it entirely, and absorb a huge amount of everyone's energy that could be spent much more productively. They have to go.

> part of owning the journey is removing the people who are consistently blocking progress

Imperative Two: difficult choices must be made

We have a lot to say about Imperative Two because the point is not only that difficult choices must be made but also that you cannot make them all yourself. That means you need to become skilled at leading debate and managing conflict. We suggest some ways you can do this, without simply imposing your will.

Making choices

Making a long list of MWBs can be easy, but making a shortlist is always much more difficult. Focus means choice, and when the MWB choices are made, some people will lose. The losers usually see their favorite projects cut or eliminated, and budgets redirected to other areas of the business. Naturally, they are resentful. As a result the tendency of some leaders is to avoid the hard choices and minimize the number of losers.

But avoiding hard choices is a mistake. Although you need to make sure everyone is heard, selecting and implementing MWBs is neither a democratic process nor a popularity contest. It is not sufficient for the leader to say, "Well, if the group agrees that these are the MWBs, then that is OK with me." The leader's job is not to find a quick consensus – a lowest common denominator to which everyone can agree. There will be times when you have to make tough decisions and disappoint some people – maybe even most people.

Clearly, the leader of an MWB journey needs to be skilled in managing debate and conflict, and we will say more about this shortly. The key is to keep the "losers" on board, and as emotionally committed to delivering success in the MWBs as everyone else. You especially need to ensure when you move from the kick-off event back to the office that these managers will show solidarity with the group decisions, and whole-heartedly lead their part of the organization in supporting the chosen MWBs. If the losers go back to the organization and say to their people, "We lost, the group made a stupid choice, there is no way we will help them," you clearly have a problem. Private conversations with such resisters may turn things around, but if these fail, your best course of action is to remove them and move on.[1]

A final suggestion is that you create and observe a "75 percent rule." You may have a strong sense of what the appropriate MWBs for the business should be, even before the kick-off event. However, leaders who impose their will, insisting that their answers are the right answers, will never get the full emotional commitment of the group. There has to be a willingness to let go of preconceived ideas and engage

---

[1] In our experience, even when someone comes on board at this point, if they remain reluctant, the level of commitment you need may never be there. While it is tempting to avoid the tough decisions in the short term, in the long run this will be more painful for everyone.

in genuine dialog with the team. In other words the leader has to be willing to actively listen, engage themselves in the process, and be open to a change of mind. Our experience suggests that when entering an initial MWB kick-off event many leaders will be able to predict the outcome in terms of the list of MWBs with about 75 percent accuracy. However, the insights gained and contributions made in devising the other 25 percent are significant in two regards. First, genuine involvement in the creation of the MWBs by the team – as opposed to leading them to preconceived answers – is critical to the team owning the resulting outputs. Second, many leaders are surprised how much they still have to learn from their own teams when they genuinely listen and engage in a dialog with them. Hence the 75 percent rule. Be prepared to yield where appropriate. Your willingness to concede will be an example to other resisters. Remember, you will be doing well if you are 75 percent right!

Leading debate and managing conflict

"Truth over harmony" is a phrase coined by Bossidy and Charan,[2] and we think it is an excellent motto for your MWB journey. Get the truth onto the table, even if it hurts. Of course, one person's version of the truth will differ from another's, so your MWB journey should generate lots of debate. Understand from the outset that disagreement is a necessary and healthy part of the journey, and do not try to suppress it. If you have no disagreements, it probably means that you are not engaging in a deep enough debate, or your managers have concluded that what is going on during the MWB process doesn't mean anything and will never result in real action. The key is to manage disagreement, focus on the collective benefits to be gained, and keep the process moving forward.

From time to time emotions will run high and at some point in the process, a crisis is likely. These crises are often turning points that break through emotional log jams, get things out in the open, and after the crisis the group is often infused with a new and more positive spirit. During these crises, "time-outs" to allow personal reflection on what has happened are essential. This is when overnight stays or outside hikes are useful. A break in time or place helps people focus on the constructive aspects of the dialog – the "truth" – and step back from

[2] Bossidy, Larry and Charan, Ram with Burck, Charles (2002) *Execution: The Discipline of Getting Things Done*, Random House Business Books, London.

the elements that they have found personally threatening. There are real advantages to holding your kick-off event in an unusual setting, and for at least three or four days. They may seem like administrative details, but location and duration do matter.

Location and duration matter

Kick-off events in unusual locations work much better than those in boardrooms or local conference facilities because they send the message from the outset that the conversations and debates are going to be out of the ordinary. Of course, you do not have to go to a mountain top – although we have certainly found that an "outdoor" element in the choice of location can help. (Unilever's team kicked off their MWB journey in the rainforests of Costa Rica, while Carlsberg's team started out in the mountains of Megève.) Walking and talking in a setting that encourages the group to look at a new or inspiring environment usually encourages deeper, more emotionally engaging conversations. Unusual stimuli produce unusual conversations.

Kick-off events usually last four or five days. The reason is that surfacing emotions takes time and you don't want people running for the safety of "home" immediately – keep them in the unusual environment to absorb and reflect, and then re-engage with the team once they have worked through their emotions and challenges. Shorter events can lead to a loss of momentum and it may take much longer to achieve what can be accomplished in a five-day event, if indeed you get there at all. Nonetheless, if there are good reasons to have shorter events, we strongly advise that the group stays overnight for at least one night, to ensure some meaningful conversations outside "office hours." Another ground rule we have found useful is that there should not be any contact with the office during the kick-off event.

As we talked to Jan about his ability to lead debates and manage conflict, he described himself as a "recovering commander," meaning that his instincts were to dominate, but he was working hard to listen to others more, and be a little more patient. (We talk of "commanders" and other management styles later in the chapter.) He told us of a debate he had presided over in his previous job at Strand. He did not think he had handled it very well.

I had been heading the Strand division for about three years and was pretty happy with my senior guys. We were not what you would call a high-performance team, but we had decent working relationships, and there was a fair level of trust among us. The division was global, and we were doing well in most parts of the world, but we were weak in Asia, and that was where the growth was going to be.

About a year ago, we agreed on an Asian strategy that would require a significant investment in Thailand. We identified two potential joint venture partners – one Japanese and one Korean – who were interested in investing in Thailand with us. The Japanese were suggesting a two-stage alliance. During the first stage there would be some benefit to Strand, but much more to the Japanese company. The second stage – two years later – looked like it would give us exactly the benefits we were seeking, but the Japanese would only start stage two, which they saw as risky, following a successful stage one.

The Korean company, on the other hand, was already a joint venture partner of ours in Korea, so we knew them fairly well. They were definitely keen to invest with us in Thailand, but we were not sure if they had the right skills. Plus, if we went with them we would invest more up front than if we went with the Japanese.

Our team met to discuss all this in London. We spent the first few hours discussing the benefits of using a joint venture and setting up an Asian base quickly. Then we got into the merits of the two joint venture proposals. The first issue on the table was the trustworthiness of the Japanese partner. Sato, the only Japanese member of my group and the country manager for Japan, got heavily involved, which was unusual for him. He argued, "This is an honorable Japanese company. Stage two of the deal will happen as they say it will. We can trust them, and we should accept their proposal."

However Ken, my Korean country manager, sharply disagreed. He did not believe that the Japanese company should be trusted – and was strongly in favor of going with the Korean partner. On paper, the Japanese partner suited our needs better – but the trust issue was huge. The Koreans had told Ken that they had worked with the Japanese company in the past, and they definitely could not be trusted. Of course, the rest of us were somewhat dubious about this information.

There was no question that Sato knew the Japanese company better than any of us, even though two of us had been talking to senior managers in this company on and off for a couple of years. And I thought Sato had our interests at heart, but I did not know how much his view reflected the fact that he was Japanese, and he was defending, in a sense, the honor of the managers in the Japanese company.

I found it very difficult to read Sato. He does not speak out very much. I guess that is typical of Japanese, but also, he found English difficult. I know that he often saw things differently from me, and sometimes brought up issues that I did not think important. In general he was more relationship oriented and more positive about alliances than most of us.

What it boiled down to was this: on the one hand, if the Japanese were sincere we would, together, be an unbeatable force in this region in five to eight years. If they were not, by going with them we would have stalled our expansion into Asia, while the Japanese gained at our expense. The Koreans, on the other hand, probably could be trusted, but we were less sure of their competence in this product area.

Jan's story is a classic example of disagreement in a senior management group. Part of the discussion was based on rational calculation – Asia is important, we are in trouble in Asia, we have to invest there, Thailand is the best choice, and we need a partner. Those parts were easy to agree. But another part of the issue was emotional. Sato was saying: "I am Japanese. You can trust me. And you can trust this Japanese potential partner." And Ken had an emotional commitment to the Korean partner, and wanted them to get the deal.

Many of Jan's team were siding with Sato, not because they thought going with the Japanese was necessarily the better deal, but stage one of the Japanese option was going to require fewer resources than the Korean alliance, and that could mean more money and engineering time for their own initiatives. So going with the Japanese partner was the most popular solution. But for the wrong reason.

Jan's third option was to set aside both the Japanese and Korean alternatives and go back to the beginning to investigate questions like "Is Thailand really the right base for us in Asia? Do we really want to use a JV?" and so on. This line of inquiry would have brought groans from almost everyone in the room, and each manager would have resisted being involved in the strategic reassessment. So in total, each option had at least two managers opposed to it, and whichever Jan chose would strain some relationships. Like many commanders, however, Jan was impatient, and did not want the debate to drag on for ever. He explained:

We had to make a decision. Getting to grips with the Japanese issue was vital, but talking to the Japanese again myself would never answer the fundamental question of trust. So I was very frustrated with Sato's inability to fully articulate his position. I started to push him hard and at one point I lost my temper, saying, "If you want us to trust these people you really have to say more than 'we should trust them because they are Japanese.'" At that point he retreated and seemed to say, OK, never mind – he seemed too intimidated to argue with me. He even said OK, let's go with the Koreans. And in my frustration, that is what we did. But I still do not know if it was the right decision, nor do I know if Sato had more information that he could have given us if I hadn't exploded at him.

Understand the sources of differences of opinion

The conflict in Jan's group stemmed from the fact that everyone had different information, different opinions, and a differing stake in the outcome of the decision regarding the joint venture partner. The situation was made more difficult by differences in language and culture, and clearly Jan's inability to keep his emotions in check only made the situation worse.

We suggest three basic steps for managers like Jan, who are trying to resolve a dispute that has important consequences for the business.

1. Try to ensure that everyone in the group has the same information.

2. Once everyone has the same information, find out whether some people are attaching markedly different probabilities of success to a proposed course of action than are others.

3. Determine the payoffs of success and penalties of failure of the proposed course of action for each member of the team, as these differences may reveal why the differences of opinion exist.

This three-stage progression will lead you from a relatively safe intellectual discussion about information through assessments of probabilities of success and then into the deeper emotional waters of the personal consequences of success and failure.

If the three steps do not help to resolve the situation, there is one further step, which is to consider whether or not the dispute is being driven by jealousy, personal rivalry, or distrust between some of the executives involved in the process. This possibility may not become a matter of public discussion, but could form the basis for one-on-one sessions between the leader and various members of the team.

1. Do some members of the group have different information from others?

Typically each executive engaging in an MWB process arrives with a different knowledge base from the others. This is a natural result of their job history and their current job as well as their broader life history – where they grew up, what education they gained, and so on. The newer the management team, the more likely it is that they will be entering the MWB process with different information. If a management team have been together a long time, they may have similar knowledge (and opinions). This can be dangerous, and in such a case there is a strong argument to be made for including some newcomers to the company, or more junior people, in the MWB process.

To resolve differences of opinion, begin by getting everyone's relevant knowledge out into the open. At issue may be knowledge about a particular company, a part of the world, a product line, or maybe a particular functional expertise. This information exercise will not be as straightforward as simply compiling information – some facts are "softer" than others. A "fact" to one executive may be an "opinion" to the rest of the group. And as we mentioned earlier, if you are a "commander" in style you may have difficulty getting your managers to venture any information, while if you are a "motivator" who does not like to hear bad news, the information you get may be filtered or biased.

Of course, you can spend the rest of your life trying to track down and verify "facts" (a potential weakness of a leader who is a "thinker") and the leader needs to decide when the group has done enough information collection and verification. Clearly, it is impossible to eliminate all ambiguity, but if there is a key fact that we do not know but should be able to find out, it may be worth taking the time to do so.

Getting all the knowledge out in the open may not resolve your dispute, but it is a necessary first step, to provide a framework for the rest of the discussion.

2. Do some members of the group attach a different probability of success to a particular course of action than the rest of the group? If so, why?

At this point the conversation may start to get more difficult, and more emotional. At a very basic level some people are more optimistic than others, some are more prone to avoid risk, and some are more open to new ideas, while others will defend the status quo rigidly. These underlying factors may not show up directly, but when you begin to discuss your firm's ability to develop a new product in a certain time frame, lower costs by a certain amount, or move faster than a particular competitor, the differences will usually start to emerge.

In Strand's case the executive in charge of research had made some rather pessimistic judgments about how long it would take to develop a variant of a Strand product that would be required for the Asian market, and that was one of the factors that had driven the group to look for an alliance partner. Several other managers, including Jan, wondered whether he was being too pessimistic.

But disregarding or overriding the opinion of an expert is a tricky business. It becomes a question of the expert's track record – is he always too conservative and just needs to be given the challenge or does he err on the side of being too optimistic? In these situations the leader has a big advantage if he has an intimate knowledge of the executive making the judgment. In Jan's case, a one-on-one discussion with the head of research led him to the decision that he should trust the researcher's judgment. He commented at the time: "To say it is a question of trust is a bit too simple. I do trust that he has the best interest of the business at heart – but I needed to make sure that he did not have an unconscious pessimistic bias about this development question. I was also worried that he might be covering up the fact that he felt that a group of his people were not up to the job. That turned out not to be the case."

When facing differences of opinion like this, we have found it useful to ask the members of the group to write down the probability of success of a particular course of action and explain their reasoning to the group. This tends to focus the discussion, and cut through the rhetoric. Often, people are amazed at how similar their estimates are, even though they are arguing different sides of the issue. What you may end up with is two groups agreeing that the probability of success is 70 percent but one group argues, that means we should go for it, while the other states the opposite. One reason for this may be that the consequences of success and failure will not fall equally across the group.

3. Are the consequences of success and failure asymmetric?

The payoff from any successful course of action will often be greater for one executive, or group of executives, than another. For example, the head of Asia in your company may want to engage in a MWB that will result in a massive increase in the company's presence in Asia. The head of R&D may be equally excited about an MWB that will increase R&D spending and staffing for his department. Everyone comes to the table with their own agenda. Some will be more visible than others, and some managers will be thinking about their personal payoff, while others will be thinking more of the benefit for the business. As the leader, you need to work on surfacing these agendas so they can be addressed.

In the case of Strand, Sato was closest to the situation in Japan, and he clearly knew more about it than the others in the management team. But that did not necessarily make his judgment more reliable. Often the person closest to the situation has the most to gain or lose by the group's decision. Sato's judgment about the Japanese company, for example, might have been consciously or unconsciously colored by a desire to do a deal with a prestigious Japanese firm, which would increase his local stature. Or perhaps he wanted to prove his worth to his Western bosses by recommending a course of action which would make him more important inside Strand.

4. Are personal factors, such as rivalry, jealousy, and distrust, at play?

Most managers are competitive individuals, which is one of the reasons they rose through the organization to become managers. And while we have stressed throughout this book that as the leader you need to insist on people thinking of the business and the group first, setting aside their individual preferences, you will never achieve this completely. Some of the debates you encounter, while cloaked as intellectual discussions, may in reality be based on one executive's jealousy of another, personal rivalry, or distrust.

Dealing with such issues during a kick-off event will probably require private conversations with the individuals involved. You will have to be very firm, and if you are unsuccessful, again you may have to make changes in the team. Competition between executives is normal, and to a certain extent healthy, but you need to channel that competitive energy into productive uses.

In Strand's case, a complication beyond "protecting turf " was that none of the team knew Sato well. Having to trust the judgment of a colleague whom you do not know well on issues that could impact the overall success of the business, and ultimately your own remuneration or position, is difficult. This is why we emphasize that throughout the MWB journey you should create as many opportunities as possible to allow the team to build strong personal relationships and as high a level of trust as possible. The more trust you can build, the easier it will be to focus on collective goals.

PS: don't avoid or ignore diversity

Building trust in managent teams, especially in an international organization like Jan's, often requires bridging gaps in understanding that result from the diverse backgrounds of the managers sitting around the table. By definition, a diverse team is one that is comprised of people who do not all think the same way, possibly because of nationality, age, gender, education, or job history, which means that differences of opinion are more likely, and probably more difficult to resolve. Certainly it is easier to lead a team in which there is a low level of diversity.

But the highest-performing teams are incredibly diverse.[3] They use their diversity to make better-informed decisions and to create commitment across organizational boundaries. So if you have a high level of ambition for your team, do not surround yourself with a low-diversity team just to make your life easier. Firmly etched on our minds are the two days we spent with an all-white, male, middle-aged, English-speaking management team of twenty people plotting the five-year future of their business. After a day of intense intellectual debate, everyone agreed that the future lay in Asia. The target was set: 25 percent of overall company revenue and profit had to come from Asia within ten years. (The current level was about 7 percent.) After a night's sleep the group reconvened and were still of the same opinion. Money that some had wanted for projects in Europe and the US was going to be diverted to Asia. Everyone, even the "losers," felt it was the right thing to do.

---

[3] As are the lowest-performing teams. For more on the research findings see DiStefano, Joseph J. and Maznevski, Martha L. (2000) "Creating value with diverse teams in global management," *Organizational Dynamics*, Vol. 29, No. 1, pp. 45–63.

For this business, at this time, Asia probably was an appropriate priority. The problem with this discussion, however, was that it was a high-level, intellectual, rational debate. No one was actually emotionally committed to the answer. Over lunch, it became increasingly clear that none of these executives wanted to be personally involved in the new initiative. All had good reasons why they could not "at the moment" move to the region. Asia was, on a personal level, "too foreign" for them. No one spoke a language other than English. No one had lived in Asia. The team was insufficiently diverse.

Dealing with diversity: map, bridge, integrate

Our IMD colleagues Martha Maznevski and Joe DiStefano suggest a three-step process for dealing with individual differences. They call the three steps "map, bridge, and integrate."

1. Map: understand the differences. Our natural tendency is to ignore differences in the way people assess information, interpret events, judge others, and so on. But focusing only on commonalities within the group will lead to lowest common denominator solutions. So instead of ignoring differences, explore them. Understand that those differences offer opportunities for innovation, creativity, and higher performance.

2. Bridge: communicate across the differences. The key here is to create an environment in which members of your team are motivated to understand each other's point of view. They must believe that by working together and really understanding each other, they can all win. Once people truly understand each other, you can look for common ground.

3. Integrate: build on the differences for high performance. Now that everyone understands everyone else, push to get the best ideas out on the table, and begin to build on those ideas. This is not unusual advice, but the difference is that having done the first two steps you will be having an open and honest conversation that takes full advantage of diversity, rather than ignoring it, or pretending it does not exist.

For more detail on the MBI process, see Maznevski, Martha L. and DiStefano, Joseph J. (2004) "Synergy from individual differences: map, bridge and integrate," *IMD Perspectives for Managers*, Issue no. 108, March.

So if you are leading an MWB journey, you need to learn to deal with debate that stems from diversity in your team – not create a team which has no diversity!

If you think that your group lacks diversity, consider inviting a few "outsiders" to the kick-off event. These might be younger managers, topic specialists, or even executives from major customers. Specialists and important customers will bring new points of view to debates, and in a few hours can explain a topic on which most managers are not up to speed. Examples might include the company's position in China, its inability to serve a particular market segment, or the vulnerability of its intellectual property rights. These specialists make their input, which may have been agreed in advance with the CEO, answer questions, and then depart.

Including younger company managers in the kick-off event has the added benefits of broadening the ownership of the decisions reached, and in the eyes of younger managers who do not attend, legitimize the whole process because some of their friends and peers were there and were heard.

Imperative Three: a team must be created

Even as you may be upsetting some of your managers during the kick-off event by insisting that "contradictory" perspectives are fully considered and tough choices are made, you have to begin the process of turning the group into a team. As we said in Chapter 2, this is not easy to do with managers at the best of times, so it can be particularly difficult in the context of a kick-off event. But such an event also offers opportunities. It is abundantly clear that business as usual and maintaining the status quo are not what the group is here to discuss. Because you have removed people from their traditional support systems and environment, there will be a feeling of loss for some, and they will need to rebond with something – and that something can be the team, with you as its leader.

Creating a real team, with fully engaged members, means that joining the team must be an attractive proposition. People should join voluntarily, even enthusiastically, not with the feeling that they are being coerced. You want active followers, people who are willing to argue with you, not passive minds who will do only what they are told. It is a fine line – you need a team of people willing to debate and engage fully, but at the end of the day each person needs to know when to stop pushing an argument that is getting no support, and join the rest of the group to create an agreed way forward.

To make the idea of working as a team attractive, start by focusing on the future. Identify shared goals. Ask the group, what do we, as a group, want to achieve? What kind of organization do we want? Do not be afraid of framing questions in an emotional way. Try questions such as: what legacy do we want to leave? What kind of organization would you be proud to create for the generation of executives who come after us? Would you want your children to work here?

joining the team must be an attractive proposition

These conversations get people thinking beyond their self-interest. The question becomes "what is best for us?" not "what is best for me?" Once people accept that group goals are important, you are well on your way toward instilling a sense of team accountability. If a battle is won, we all win. If a battle is lost, we all lose. So, even if you are in a neighboring silo, or fighting a different MWB from the one I am primarily engaged in, my question is: how can I help you? The job of the leader is to create shared meaning and shared responsibility within the group.

The first key test of your progress in building a management team usually comes toward the end of the kick-off event, when you ask all participants to make a personal statement of their commitment to the chosen MWBs and to commit to new behaviors to support the group. It is at this point that the realities of interdependence hit home. "I am really going to have to depend on these guys to get things done. Can I trust them?" This is a scary feeling, particularly if you do not know your colleagues well. Naturally, questions spring into executives' minds: who will win the political battles? Will someone else get the credit for my work? How will this impact my career? Why should I try new approaches – and if I do, what if my colleagues won't? Should I really put the interests of the collective ahead of my own?

These entirely reasonable doubts make the first weeks and months back at work vital. Were the promises made at the kick-off event real, or just a passing dream? It depends on you, the leader, to make sure that the fine words and promises turn into actions. Which begs the following question . . .

Is there a "best" management style for leading an MWB journey?

No, there is no single "best" management style for leading an MWB journey. But if you want to turn your management group into a team while you are en route, we do have some advice. We believe that successful MWB leadership requires flexibility – the capacity to use a variety of styles, and to recognize when each is appropriate. So while you undoubtedly have a preferred style with which you are most comfortable, there will be times when you should behave differently. If you are by nature a "commander" (see below), for example, who likes to take charge and stay in charge, there will be occasions when you should back off, listen, let others have the floor, and even carry the day with their arguments. You need to know when to let go, and when to assert leadership, which may mean deciding that a debate has gone on long enough, and forcing resolution on a contentious issue.

In fact you may need to use different styles with different members of your team, especially in small group or one-on-one discussions. Bear in mind that as you enter the kick-off event, some people will be much less comfortable than others. For some, the process will challenge their loyalties, existing relationships, status, and ways of thinking. And since what you are promising in return is nothing more than the possibility of a better future, it is not surprising that they will have an initial, and perhaps continuing, reluctance to fully engage in the MWB process. Others will see a compelling need for change and fully believe in the MWB journey, wishing it had happened sooner. You have to work with both groups. Sometimes you will have to be a diplomat, sometimes a motivator, at other times a thinker or maybe a commander. The critical skill is recognizing the situations in which each style is appropriate.

There are four management styles that we come across frequently during MWB journeys.[4] They are described below, together with advice to leaders who prefer each style.

[4] These are our own definitions, drawing on many of the excellent leadership and management-style descriptions available. If you would like to investigate your leadership or management style in more depth, there are a number of institutions which offer diagnostic tools, including: Center for Creative Leadership (*www.ccl.org*), Personnel Decisions International (PDI) (*www.personneldecisions.com*), Development Dimensions International (*www.ddiworld.com*), and Emerging Leaders (*www.emergingleaders.com.au*).

The commander[5]

If you are a commander you know the right answers and do not need a lot of input from the rest of the management team. You are sure of your opinions, and decisive. A one-man show. The rest of the team may or may not be comfortable with your style. Good people may have been driven away as they realized their opinions were not valued or, if the business has been very successful, people may have stayed because of the exhilaration that has accompanied the success. Many entrepreneurs are commanders.

The commander style is not likely to work well in an MWB setting, as the process is built on the assumption that listening to others on the management team is, on average, likely to lead to better decisions, and better implementation of those decisions. The exception is if the business is in crisis and decisions have to be made quickly; building the commitment of the management team is not a major challenge, as people will work to save the business and their jobs. Our advice to commanders is to:

- Encourage others to offer their opinions. But do not be surprised if they are hesitant to do so, as you do not usually ask for their input. When management team members begin to speak up, do not be harshly critical or dismissive when their opinions or conclusions differ from your own.

- Avoid using the power of your position or force of personality to win the argument, especially when disagreements persist. As we said earlier, begin to explore differences by making sure that everyone has the same information and then lead a discussion of everyone's assessments of the probabilities of success, based on that information. When others' assessments differ from your own, listen!

- Be as patient as you can. Most commanders are impatient. If you see yourself as surrounded by people less competent than yourself, ask yourself why. For you one of the most challenging aspects of the MWB process will be to develop your management group into a team.

---

[5] This particular style and label was drawn from the work of our colleague, Paul Strebel, on trajectory management. Please see Strebel, Paul (2003) *Trajectory Management: Leading a Business Over Time*, J. Wiley and Sons, UK.

The diplomat

As a diplomat you are very aware that your management team is composed of a diverse set of individuals, each with different interests and degrees of influence. You know who the key players are, and where they stand on critical issues. In Goleman's[6] terms you are very high on social networking skills – the ability to find areas of agreement and build consensus. In a kick-off event the diplomat will be very good at knowing when to go "offline" and work with people one on one, and when to reconvene the group as a whole. The diplomat will also know when to appeal to her team's rational, intellectual side and when to appeal to emotions. The good news about this management style is that consensus is usually reached and the group moves forward. The danger is that the diplomat's process may be centered more on avoiding conflict and building consensus than finding the best way forward for the business. Our advice:

● Diplomats tend to breed political decision-making processes. Try to add objectivity. Consider ideas independent of who suggested them. Do not listen only to the most influential people. Listen to and encourage the quiet voices, as they may have the expertise that the business needs.

● Do not always go for the quick consensus. Ask yourself what is best for the business, not just what will get the fastest or easiest agreement.

The thinker

Thinkers take in a lot of input from others on the team. They are data driven, and the way to influence a thinker is to do your homework well. Half-baked ideas will not survive very long. Numbers are important. The worst type of thinking leaders are those who cannot stop looking for a perfect solution and move forward to make a decision. These are leaders who come up with the "ideal" decision six months too late. Another thing that separates effective and ineffective thinking leaders is whether or not they pay attention to the emotional side of their

[6] See Goleman, Daniel (1996) *Emotional Intelligence*, Bloomsbury Publishing, Great Britain; the domains of emotional intelligence were updated in Goleman, Daniel, Boyatzis, Richard, and McKee, Annie (2002) *Primal Leadership*, Harvard Business School Publishing, USA. We discuss emotional intelligence further a little later in this chapter.

decisions. Some focus only on the "rational," others are very aware of the emotional side of the MWB process. Our advice:

● Do not assume that you are the only one capable of thinking on the management team. When you ask others for data, also ask them for their conclusions and judgments based on the data.

● Do not strive for perfect answers. Remember the 80–20 rule: twenty percent of the data will get you 80 percent of the answer. Timing does matter – make a decision and move forward: you will learn more as you go.

The motivator

If you are a motivator you are by nature an optimist. The future is seen as a place of opportunity and you believe your task is to inspire your followers to seize that future aggressively. Obstacles are by nature surmountable, and speed is good because if the future is going to be great, the sooner we get there the better. Negative or cautionary comments from members of the management team are not welcome. Nor are business plans that are seen as insufficiently ambitious. The danger of the motivational style of management is that reality may be ignored. One of the most visible American motivators is John Chambers, CEO of Cisco, who, before the company's crash in early 2001, "believed in the myth of unstoppable growth."[7] Belief in the business and its future is important, of course, but so is facing up to what Jim Collins calls the "brutal facts."[8] Our advice:

● What is motivating in one culture may not be in another. So be careful of cultural differences. A team of British managers are unlikely to be motivated by the same rhetoric as a team of American managers.

● Do not shoot the messenger. If it is career threatening to deliver bad news to the boss, no one will do it. The result will be a leader increasingly cut off from reality.

---

[7] Slater, Robert (2003) *The Eye of the Storm: How John Chambers Steered Cisco Through the Technology Collapse*, HarperBusiness, USA, p. 239.
[8] Collins, Jim (2001) *Good to Great*, Random House Business Books, UK. In the book Jim Collins devotes a whole chapter (Chapter 4) to exploring this issue in depth. In particular we note the Stockdale Paradox: "Retain faith that you will prevail in the end, regardless of the difficulties. *And at the same time* confront the most brutal facts of your current reality, whatever they might be."

- If you have to spend a lot of time motivating your management team, you probably have the wrong people.

Does emotional intelligence matter?

You will have noticed that most of this advice centers on so-called "soft" issues around managing yourself and others. There is a good reason for this. Much has been written in recent years about the need for leaders to demonstrate what Daniel Goleman[9] calls "emotional intelligence." Goleman argues that superior intelligence is not enough to make a great leader. Leaders need what he calls emotional intelligence, which is comprised of four "domains":

1. Self-awareness.

2. Self-management.

3. Social awareness.

4. Relationship management.

We agree. Emotional intelligence[10] is indeed important for managers leading an MWB journey. The box below discusses the implications for managers leading an MWB process of each of the four domains that Goleman and his colleagues have identified.

[9] Goleman, Daniel (1996) *Emotional Intelligence*, Bloomsbury Publishing, Great Britain; the domains of emotional intelligence were updated in Primal Leadership, Daniel Goleman, Richard Boyatzis and Annie McKee (2002), Harvard Business School Publishing, USA.
[10] The Emotional Intelligence Consortium (*www.eiconsortium.org*) offers tools for assessing emotional intelligence.

Emotional intelligence and MWB leadership

The domains of emotional intelligence	Implications for MWB leaders
Self-awareness Goleman et al. ("Goleman") argue that the ability to recognize one's moods and emotions and their impact on others is the foundation of emotional intelligence, and the hallmark of a good leader.	This recommendation has definite applicability to the MWB process. Because many leaders embark on the MWB process when they are unhappy with the performance of the business (and their managers), they may enter the process in a negative, scolding mood, ready to cast blame on their team members for a wide variety of faults. This, needless to say, is not a productive mind set if the objective is to get people engaged in an open process of sharing ideas and possibilities. Our advice would be to look forward, not backward. The MWB process must be more about creating a positive future than deciding who is to blame for a less than stellar past or present.
Goleman also suggests that good leaders should know their own strengths and weaknesses.	If you are the CEO of a business you are probably already aware of where your strengths lie, and to cover your weaknesses we would suggest that you share the leadership of the MWB process. For example, if you are not by nature numerically oriented, have your CFO lead some sessions. If you tend to be impatient, have someone else lead certain sessions where you suspect your patience will be stretched beyond breaking point. Bringing others into leadership positions will not hurt your position and should enhance the overall process.

The domains of emotional intelligence	Implications for MWB leaders
Self-management Here Goleman is talking about the ability to control yourself and avoid inappropriate spontaneous reactions. In other words, you need the ability to think before acting because emotions are contagious.	This is much easier to do in an MWB process if you are not always standing in front of the group, and can be a major reason for using a facilitator. You can sit as a participant and think over your interventions before you make them. Goleman's advice does not mean that you should be without emotions. No one will be impressed if you appear overly controlled, hiding what you think, and not entering fully into debates. But do be particularly careful of negative outbursts, especially if they are aimed at specific individuals. Such explosions of emotion usually do more harm than good, and it will take some time to recover and get back on track.
Social awareness This is the ability to understand the emotional make-up of other people and to be sensitive to their feelings when you are making decisions or moving into action. It includes the ability to read networks and decision flows effectively, managing rather than being hampered by politics.	These are definitely valuable attributes for an MWB leader, especially with a diverse, multicultural group. But such sensitivity (or empathy) can be a double-edged sword. If you truly take everyone's feelings into account, you may never do anything. Or if you try to choose a course of action that will create the least hurt among team members, you will probably make some bad decisions. Our advice is to not do things that will needlessly hurt people as you go through the process. When you are making arguments for or against particular MWBs, leave certain personal things unsaid if that will help, do not directly attack anyone, and do not rub the "losers'" faces in the fact that they have lost, and prevent others from doing so as well.

▶

The domains of emotional intelligence	Implications for MWB leaders
Social awareness (cont.)	This all seems very obvious, but there are many examples of such things happening as emotions get high.
Relationship management When Goleman speaks of relationship skills, he means the ability to influence others, build rapport, and find common ground for moving forward.	There can be no doubt that influencing skills are a definite asset for the MWB leader. The use of effective rhetoric, logic, numerical arguments, diagrams, stories, simple metaphors, and analogies to other situations can all be very powerful. Because different team members will find different types of argument more compelling, we suggest that you use a variety of approaches. Some people prefer numbers and tight logic; others like metaphors and symbols. Use both.
Managing relationships effectively also means inspiring and motivating people.	You and your team are going to have to face the "brutal facts" as you go through your MWB process, and there will undoubtedly be times when the group becomes despondent about the future. "We are in the wrong markets with the wrong products, and have none of the capabilities that we will need in the future" is a familiar refrain. At such times you need to display a strong belief in the future of the business. As the old saying goes, "Things are never as good, nor as bad, as they seem." It is your job to remind everyone of that and to demonstrate it with your personal energy. Show optimism, even when things get tough.

Can you take the heat and the grief?

You will certainly need a strong dose of emotional intelligence during your MWB journey, but we are in agreement with Ronnie Heifetz when he argues that emotional intelligence skills are "necessary but not sufficient" for great leadership. He believes that leaders also need the courage to raise tough questions and sometimes to go against the flow.[11] He wrote:

> Emotional intelligence is necessary for leadership but not sufficient. Leadership couples emotional intelligence with the courage to raise the tough questions, challenge people's assumptions about strategy and operations – and risk losing their goodwill. It demands a commitment to serving others; skill at diagnostic, strategic and tactical reasoning; the guts to get beneath the surface of tough realities; and the heart to take the heat and grief.

MWB leaders may need to demonstrate courage in a variety of ways: courage to ask questions that you know no one wants to hear; courage to support a manager that no one wants you to support; courage to trust others; courage to take on the whole group when you are very sure they are wrong; and the courage to yield. You are certainly going to need Goleman's recommended skills, but there will be times when a thick skin and the guts to go against the flow are much more the order of the day. The trick is to know when.

As a final note, we should point out that in most cases the heat and grief continue as the journey progresses. So you have to be tenacious, constantly pushing toward the vision and overcoming multiple obstacles. You need the courage to keep asking those unwelcome questions; to keep trusting others even when you are itching to take the reins yourself; to keep energizing your team, even when you are reaching deep into your own reserves to keep going. You have to carry on listening actively, making sure people can contribute meaningfully and focusing on possibilities and opportunities, not pitfalls.

[11] Heifetz, Ronald (2004) "Leading by feel," *Harvard Business Review*, January, p. 37. Ronald Heifetz is a co-founder of the Center for Public Leadership at Harvard University's John F. Kennedy School of Government in Cambridge, Massachusetts, and a partner at Cambridge Leadership Associates, a consultancy in Cambridge.

Are you ready to own the journey?

We end this chapter where we began, with the question of ownership. Now that you have a better sense of what an MWB journey demands of its leader, do you want the job? Could you own such a journey? The key questions, similar to those at the end of Chapter 1, but more personal, are:

1. Do you personally believe strongly that an MWB journey could have significant benefits for your business? Is the potential reward worth the effort that you will have to make?

2. Will you get enough support from your management team? Will they see the value of the journey or will they fight you all the way?

3. Are you comfortable with the idea that you will have to lead two journeys: one intellectual and one emotional? Can you deal with emotional conflict, and support the idea of "truth over harmony"?

4. Can you be flexible enough in your management style to lead the process effectively?

5. Do you have the energy to lead the journey from beginning to end? As must be apparent by now, an MWB journey is definitely not a "quick fix."

These questions are very personal. To answer them fully you need to probe your beliefs, behaviors, and readiness to change. Now, before the journey starts, you must be open with yourself. And if your responses to the questions are tentative or half-hearted, do not start on the journey, for once it starts there really is no opportunity to turn back the clock to "business as usual." You will have to be open with your team at a much more personal level than ever before, in the same way that you will be asking openness from them. Again, this can be high risk, but the rewards are potentially great for both the business and your personal development.

It did not take Jan long to conclude that he wanted to proceed with an MWB journey. Neither the business nor the management team were in good health, and something dramatic was needed to set both on a new course. Like most newly appointed managers Jan was full of energy and optimism.

He had spent time reflecting and talking with a trusted mentor about what it would require of him to lead the journey. He knew his normal, somewhat impatient leadership style would be sorely tested. He was mentally ready to lead the process, but concluded that he would need help, particularly in planning and running the kick-off event. A facilitator was engaged, on the understanding that Jan would take ownership of the process, and whenever possible the facilitator would remain in the background.

Having made the decision to move forward, Jan and the facilitator began to sort through the immediate practical decisions that had to be made about who to invite to the event, how the agenda might work, and where and when it should be. There was no benefit to waiting to start the journey because the latest quarterly figures were already hinting at the decline in sales Jan had feared in his core markets. It was time to get the rest of the team engaged.

Using external assistance

Many managers who decide to embark on an MWB journey conclude that external assistance would be useful, particularly in the early stages of the process. We have summarized below the potential benefits of working with a facilitator who has experience with MWB journeys.

Table 3.1 Potential benefits of external assistance

Stage of the journey	Potential benefits of external assistance
● Planning the overall MWB journey	● Sharing experience from previous MWB journeys.
	● Offering objectivity/anonymity for collecting or managing sensitive data and issues from the management team prior to the kick-off event.
	● Defining starting conditions and assessing the balance that will be needed between emotional and intellectual activities.
	● Coaching the leader with respect to management style and appropriate role, including thinking through potential "flashpoints" (contentious issues or difficult personalities).
	● Providing additional resources so the process can move quickly.
● The kick-off event	● Creating the exercises to be used during the kick-off event.
	● Facilitating sessions when the leader needs to be a "group member," thus allowing the leader to switch roles as needed.
	● Helping the leader decide when to move the process forward from opening windows to defining the MWBs, and then committing to one agenda.
	● Bringing a fresh perspective to the challenges/opportunities facing the business.
● Taking the journey forward	● Providing an objective assessment of progress being made, and identifying areas where energy or focus is lacking.
	● Helping to design activities to re-energize the process as needed.
	● Filling skill or content gaps.

However, there may also be disadvantages to using external assistance, including the following:

● The leader may abdicate ownership of the MWB journey – relying too much on external help. This can reduce buy-in from the team and the organization if they perceive the leader is not driving the process, or does not fully buy into it.

● External people may not be skilled enough at working with senior teams – either intervening too much, or not intervening at critical moments when they could play a useful role. In short, the external facilitator may become a burden on the leader – just one more person that he or she has to manage.

● Sensitive discussions may be inhibited by the presence of outsiders, particularly if they are too visible.

● The costs of external help may outweigh the benefits.

The benefits of using external assistance often decrease over time as the journey progresses and the MWB teams increase in number and cascade down into the organization. As everyone in the company gains more experience with the MWB process they can advise each other on the best way forward. Internal experts can become facilitators who can help others with the process.

If you do decide to use external help, we suggest the following guidelines:

1. Know what you need and when you need it. Be as clear as you can in your own mind about why you need help, what type of help you are going to need, and when you will need it.

2. Set clear ground rules for external interventions. As the leader you need to own the entire MWB journey and be seen to own it. The best facilitators are nearly invisible to the broader group. They work behind the scenes and provide input and encouragement quietly, when needed. The leader needs to agree clear ground rules with any external body ahead of time.

3. Do not be afraid to let go. It can be difficult for some leaders to "let go" of the sounding board or coach, but it is part of taking ownership. Especially after the kick-off event, the journey must be driven by the leader and the management team.

Section **II**

Engaging the team

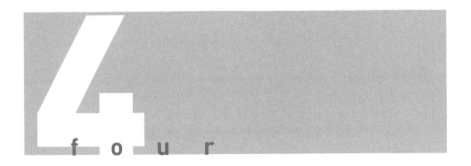

Opening windows: sharing perspectives and realities

One month later: Monday morning

Jan's management team, six men and three women, all warmly dressed, are sitting eating breakfast in the morning sunshine outside a rather basic French hotel. Conversation is speculative but muted as they take in the scenery. It feels a long way from the offices back home. They are about to begin the kick-off week of their MWB journey. No one is entirely sure how this journey will unfold, how long it will last, or what impact it will have on the company. Jan is feeling both excited and apprehensive.

Setting down his coffee cup, and looking around the table, he begins:

> Why are we here? As we start this week I want to share with you my objectives for bringing us together.

> We are clearly at a transition point. There is a fundamental reshaping occurring in our industry. Gone are the days when profitable growth came easily, and the new markets, particularly Eastern Europe, are going to be much more difficult than our home markets of the UK, France, and Germany. Key customers in our established markets are demanding more and more, while at the same time our traditional competitors are becoming increasingly aggressive. Making matters worse are the new environmental regulations that make our manufacturing and supply chain operations more complex and expensive.

In spite of this difficult environment, our target, as you know, is to double sales in Europe in five years, while increasing margins. That is ambitious, but we have to do it. Corporate is counting on us to deliver that growth.

As a leadership team we have fundamental questions to address – but as we clarify our path forward and look for new ways of working together, we should not disregard the traditions and strengths that have made us successful in the past. We need to reshape and refocus, not abandon our strengths.

We have spent a lot of time analyzing trends and developing our strategy. The purpose of this week is not to go back and re-examine this work. The challenge is for us to decide how we will add focus and clarity to our strategy and make it a reality. We need to reduce the number of initiatives we are pursuing, and put all our energy and resources behind a few battles that we absolutely must win. This week is all about creating focus and energy during a period of uncertainty, challenge, and opportunity.

This brings me to an important point. You have not been invited here because you are the head of your particular unit, you are here as a member of the executive management committee (EMC). This week is not about what "I" will do in my specific area of responsibility, it is about what we, as individuals, can collectively do to make the company successful. It is about where we are going and how we will work together. We will put aside petty quarrels and destructive ways of working. This week is not about finger pointing, it is about working together for the betterment of the company.

This does not mean that we will not address the challenges that face us. We will put many issues on the table this week, and work together to find solutions. So do raise issues, but put as much effort into listening to your colleagues and their concerns as you do into giving your own opinions. We all need to spend as much time truly listening to each other as we do talking at each other.

I have a personal request for each of you as we begin – trust the process that we have put together. We have not provided a detailed agenda for the week: it will evolve based on our discussions. We will, however, get to all of the important issues, and by Friday we will have had the difficult discussions that we need to have. But do not try to jump in at the beginning and raise all of the issues immediately. If you feel impatient, slow down and focus on the discussion at hand. Trust the process and at each point in time put all your energy into the discussion of the moment.

We have now been working together as a team for three months. We have begun to form behavior patterns and ways of working together. Now is a good time to examine where we are as a team. What is working and what is not? How can we collectively become more effective? We are beginning a journey that will last several years. To make that journey a success we will need lots of energy and a large part of that will come from the satisfaction and fun of working together.

So, this is my thinking in putting together this session. On the bus on the way here last night, you were asked to think about our hopes and fears for this week. I now want us to spend some time sharing these hopes and fears. Let's begin.

Jan had spent a lot of time thinking about his introduction. As he spoke he could already see from their body language that at least some of the group would argue it would be a "waste of time" to review things that they "already knew." He could imagine the comments: "Yes, the industry is changing; yes, we have to respond. But the way to do that is to focus on the front line, not spend a week in the middle of nowhere, navel-gazing." Jan was worried that the week could turn into an orgy of finger pointing as they all blamed each other for the company's problems. Although he had used the word "team" throughout his address Jan knew that his management group was far from being a team. He had already replaced one member of the management team and knew he might have to do so again.

It was time to start. Jan paused and looked around the table expectantly, but somewhat nervously. Was this going to work? Who would start speaking? He knew that they needed to cover both emotional issues and intellectual issues during the week, and had decided to start with the hopes and fears exercise, to put a first toe in the water on the emotional side. He wanted to use the exercise to discover what people thought the group could achieve during the week, and how they thought it could go wrong. Jan knew there were some cynics around the table and he wanted to start by bringing their doubts into the open.

The conversation began tentatively. Some people were clearly uneasy, making comments along the lines of, "I hope the weather is good," "I hope we do not have to sleep outdoors," and "I hope we are not going to do anything dangerous." (In fact, they were not going to do anything dangerous. The exercise was being held in a remote location to remove all work-related distractions and to move people beyond their usual thinking habits and patterns.) As the discussion progressed, the comments became more pointed:

> I hope we can agree on some major strategic issues, and come together as a team.

> I fear that we will all just take our usual positions, and have a conversation here in the mountains that exactly replicates one we could have held in our conference room.

> I hope this is not just a chance for Jan to shove his ideas down our throats.

Gradually people began to loosen up. Some voiced fears about how the process could go wrong; others felt that the week represented a great opportunity to move the business and the management team forward. The discussion turned to how the negative results foreseen by the doubters could be avoided. The group concluded that the key element was open and honest conversation – they all had to take the perspective of the whole business, not just their piece of it. It was decided that during the rest of the week, anyone had the right to intervene when they felt that these rules were not being followed.

Jan felt that they had made a good start, and it was now time to talk about the future of the business.

We have described Jan's opening address and his group's first, tentative discussions because his objectives and concerns are very normal for managers embarking on an MWB journey. While Jan's first objective for the week was to clarify and bring focus to the firm's strategy by identifying and agreeing on MWBs, his second and equal objective, without which the MWBs would never be won, was to transform the executive management committee into an energized leadership team. Only then would they be able to put a sustained and high level of effort behind the MWB journey and ensure that the battles would actually be won. The week in France was only the first step on a long road, but it was a vital step.

MWB building blocks

Typically, a week-long MWB kick-off event (Phase One of the journey) involves the three stages outlined in Figure 4.1. Before launching right

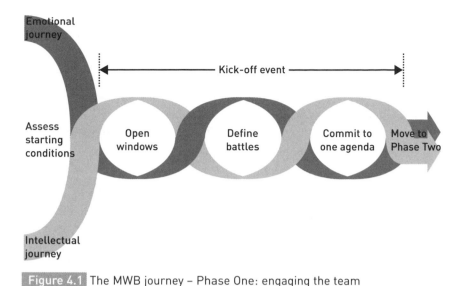

Figure 4.1 The MWB journey – Phase One: engaging the team

into the process, let's briefly revisit the "building blocks" of Phase One that were introduced in Chapter 1, and how they fit together.

The starting point of the kick-off event is to open some windows – get some fresh air into the room, if you will. You have to find a way to move beyond the conversations you have had a thousand times before, with the usual people making their same old arguments. And as we have said, the new perspectives that need to come with that fresh breeze should be both intellectual and emotional in nature.

In this chapter we describe exercises that should bring renewed energy to your team and lead them to new perspectives with respect to the others on the team, the way the leadership team operates, the organization, and the business itself. These new shared perspectives will become the foundation for making collective choices on the 3–5 MWBs that are vital to the group's future, during the portion of the kick-off event that we have labeled "Define and agree the battles: collide to decide."

The end of the week is devoted to building ownership and commitment to one shared agenda, and this is not just about priorities for the business but also about behaviors and new ways of working together. The objective is to create high levels of commitment around both aspects of the new agenda that will be transferred back to the office. The ownership of the MWBs and the new ways of working together should be obvious to all – whether they were at the kick-off event or not. As we said earlier, the success of the kick-off is not measured by how the executives feel at the end of the week, it is measured in real changes in the business that take place in the following months.

The components or "building blocks" in Figure 4.1 are common to many MWB kick-off events. But, as we described in Chapter 2, they must be customized to reflect the starting conditions of the business, team, and leader. There is no such thing as a formula for running the kick-off event, nor is there a single clear pattern of how different groups of executives move through the week. But our experience suggests that the sequence is important. Without "opening windows" first, discussions on strategic priorities will revert to the same old positions; without "colliding to decide" and making choices together there will be no basis for a shared action agenda; and without having the team "commit to one agenda" the likelihood of success back at the office diminishes. To get started, you first need some fresh air.

Opening windows

The basic premise of opening windows should now be clear. Doing it is the hard part. Most teams, particularly at the top of companies, have spent lots of time talking together. Despite this fact, most teams have surprisingly varied perspectives on their businesses and organizations and the challenges facing both. The silo effect is not just in the way many companies work, it is also in how they think. Opening the windows to break down these silos is the critical first step. Shared perspectives can lead to shared solutions, while it is only natural that individual executives with individual perspectives will have individual solutions. Without an aligned leadership team at the top, it will be difficult – if not impossible – to build the alignment down in the organization. Differences multiply as you increase the number of layers involved. The impact of self-interest and biased perspectives (logical from focusing only on one part of a business) are critical issues that must be faced.

differences multiply as you increase the number of layers involved

So what do we mean by "emotional" and "intellectual" windows?

Opening emotional windows leads to discussions about how the organization and leadership team work, not on paper but in the real day-to-day operations. Many organizations look good on paper, but actual ways of working can vary from this dramatically. Conflicts, politics, personal agendas, and just plain differences of opinion are but a few of the factors that impact how organizations operate. Without putting these issues on the table – and addressing them – they may adversely impact other decisions in the critical execution phase.

Opening intellectual windows stimulates new ways of looking at the business. If you were a financial analyst, how would you view us? What if you were a major customer? Supplier? Competitor? And so on. Where has the business been and where is it today? Do we agree on our history? The challenge is to move beyond "just data" to create shared insights about the challenges and opportunities facing the business that will give us a shared base for informed debate when we move to make our choice of MWBs.

Three core ideas underpin the process of opening windows:

1. Getting the "fish" on the table

   The most important thing as you open windows is to get the "fish on the table" and make sure everyone has a good grasp on reality, even if the discussions are painful in some cases, such as acknowledging that the team really does not operate well together. You must engage the team at an emotional as well as an intellectual level, surface the fears and cynicism that might block progress, and start to build the momentum, hopes, and aspirations that will create the energy to drive forward as the challenges and options for the business become clearer over the week.

Getting the fish on the table

Getting the fish on the table means, simply, to put on the table those important issues that everyone knows are true but no one talks about. The phrase was coined by Professor George Kohlreiser based on his memories of the Italian fish market where you could see fishermen early in the morning bringing their catches to shore. Crisp air is soon filled with a healthy fishy smell from the stalls of the merchants. Before the fish get to the waiting dinner tables they have to be cleaned. Not a pretty sight, but it must be done every morning. By noon, the smell is less appealing and cleaners come to hose the grounds and the stalls. ▶

Letting the fish fester is not a pleasant thought . . .

Below are a few examples of such "undiscussables" from MWB sessions in which we have participated:

- It is almost impossible to bring bad news to the CEO because of the ensuing negative reaction.
- A failing venture should have been shut down, but it continues because it is the CEO's pet project.
- We always go head-to-head with competitor X (and lose a lot of money in the process) because two of our management team used to work for that company, and are still trying to settle old scores.
- Executive Y makes lots of promises about cooperating with others, but never delivers.
- We pretend to make decisions in meetings like this, but the real decisions are made afterwards (or beforehand) in the CEO's office.

In most cases it is impossible to have a meaningful group discussion without getting issues like these out in the open. For the leader, this means accepting that the process may expose your weaknesses as well as those of others or the organization more broadly. The challenge is to encourage openness but not punish those brave enough to speak the truth.

2. **Promoting transparency – from data and analysis to shared insights**
   Actively sharing all the knowledge that is available on the business, the team, and the individuals who make it up allows you to harness all the "horsepower" and experience that you have in the room. Some of the information will have been prepared in advance, such as the traditional strategic analysis; some will be brought out through the exercises and debates. The objective is to get everyone on the same page in terms of understanding and being able to think about the challenges ahead in an informed way, because what the team can achieve together is greater than the sum of individual thinking.

3. **Generating shared and aligned perspectives**
   You want each team member to step out of their individual role and into a team role. This requires building new – shared – perspectives on the business, the team, and themselves. Making information transparent is a first step toward this goal, but the aim is to push this new way of looking at things further. Through exercises that

deliberately take the team out of their comfort zones and push them to experience the business (and themselves) through the eyes of other people, these new perspectives will be deepened, enriched, and aligned.

Moving on to the process itself, Figure 4.2 (overleaf) shows some of the exercises and debates we typically use at the start of the kick-off event.

The key is to let the group experience, not just talk about, different or new perspectives on the present and the future. At different points the focus is on (a) each individual – as in the "hopes and fears" exercise just discussed; (b) the management team as a group, e.g. in "how we operate as a team"; (c) the whole business, e.g. in "looking back on our success"; and (d) key industry level players and trends, e.g. in "outside-in perspectives."

There is nothing fixed about the order in which you should use these activities in a kick-off event, and you may decide to leave out a few entirely or add others of your own. Once the process is under way it will take on a life of its own, and the pieces shown in Figure 4.2 will be rearranged on the fly. It does help, however, to have the possible elements firmly in mind before starting, as you may have to make some quick judgment calls about what to do next when everyone is looking at you for leadership halfway through the second day!

The amount of time the group spends on any given item will vary enormously, and you should not try to prescribe in advance exactly how much time you will spend on each topic. The "outside-in perspectives" exercise, for example, may not take long for a group that knows its key external players very well, but could take much longer if the group is discussing, say, customer- or competitor-related issues in depth for the first time. (In such a case raw material on key customers/competitors should have been prepared in advance and supplied to the group before the session or during the week.) How much time you spend on any individual item will depend on how important that element is judged to be, and how much uncertainty surrounds it.

Below we describe how each exercise is normally used and the results that they might produce. But first, let's run through the information you will need to have collected ahead of time if you are to get the most out of the event.

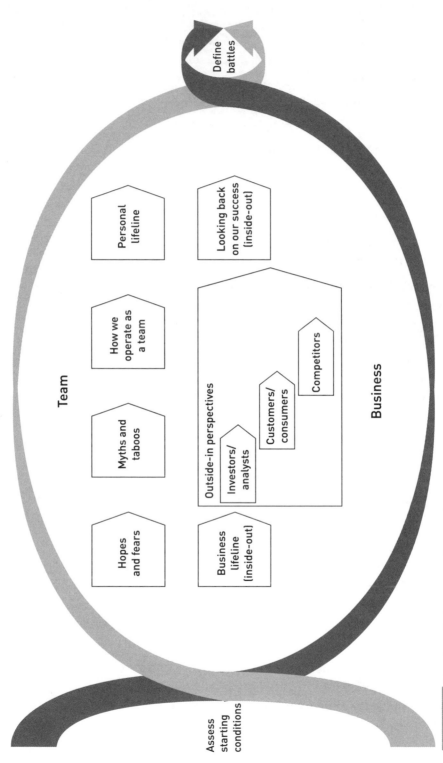

Figure 4.2 Opening windows: sample exercises

What information do you need?

Despite the lack of a definitive agenda, it is important to have a range of "concrete" information before starting the kick-off event. The reasons are twofold: to allow the team to focus on dialog and decision making rather than revisiting old arguments or searching for missing facts, and to ensure discussions do not degenerate into opinion battles. Without the necessary background information, it can be difficult to move forward. If you are not confident that you have sufficient or appropriate inputs, get them before you start the kick-off event.

To develop MWBs you need as much background information as possible on intellectual and emotional aspects of the business. But don't reinvent the wheel: pull in prior thinking on strategy, objectives, and organizational capabilities. However, recognize that there is likely to be very limited information on emotional factors. Normally the intellectual inputs are more readily available and typically include:

- Assessments of your marketplace and industry situation: most companies have a range of internal and external studies already available (often too many!).
- Your company's objectives and strategic priorities: including the hard financial and business targets set for the firm or business unit.
- A realistic and challenging assessment of the company's current and required organizational capabilities.
- Customer and consumer feedback reports.
- Competitor profiles or assessments.

MWB sessions are designed to help surface emotional issues, so you should not worry if you do not have much information ahead of time. However, more emotionally based inputs that you should bring, if you have them, include:

- Statements of vision, mission, and values – these give some basis for discussing collective ambitions for the organization (which is part of the "looking back on our success" exercise), but are unlikely to offer a comprehensive view as most statements are rational, externally focused, and short.
- Organizational culture or staff morale studies.
- Interviews/feedback from your executives on their assessment of the company's situation and challenges.

To make all this information readily available to the group at the event, the "four walls" approach is particularly useful. The idea is to make use of all the wall space you have in the main discussion room for the kick-off event to display the key pieces of information you have gathered. They can then be referred to easily as discussions and debates proceed.

Take, for example, the business unit of a major Scandinavian media company that developed posters to capture key pieces of information needed for its kick-off event, and then posted them on all four walls of the meeting room:

Wall 1: Situation assessments
> The company had multiple studies of its industry, market dynamics, and competitive positioning, some developed in house and others commissioned from various consultants. The key conclusions from each study were captured on several posters.

Wall 2: Our strategy plus independent industry assessments
> This wall captured the current strategic priorities of the business, its vision, and mission statements, plus the hard financial and operational targets that had been built into the latest budget. Alongside were summaries of the views of leading independent analysts about the industry and the various players within it, including the business unit and its parent.

Wall 3: Views of our customers and users, plus our own executives
> The company had access to a number of surveys that had been conducted among its customers and users. Summaries of the findings from these, including selected quotes, provided qualitative perspectives from the core market segments that could add richness to the conversations. In addition, a number of the executives had been interviewed about their views of the key challenges facing the company during the assessment of the starting conditions. Summaries of these views were posted on the third wall.

Wall 4: Strategic frameworks
> The aim of this wall was to provide a range of approaches for thinking about developing strategic priorities, from the classic market assessment tools to strategies for growth alternatives and approaches to driving change. These acted as "thought-starters" for the group as they looked for ways to approach the MWB selection process.

The immediate advantage of having all this information displayed on the walls, rather than in folders or binders, is that it is readily accessible and easy to incorporate in the natural flow of conversation. The participants were able to get up and point to the piece of information they were using to make a point rather than scrabbling to try to get everyone to turn to a particular page (if indeed they were able to remember which page it was on) and losing the thread of the argument. Because related information showing different perspectives was located close together, it also opened up the thinking about how different stakeholders viewed the challenges for the company – and therefore the strategic options available.

Finally, making all the information transparent – and literally immersing the group in it – helped the participants build a shared understanding of the total reality they were facing. Everyone now had the big picture, not just their own corner of it. In building this shared understanding they were also starting to take ownership of the challenges as a team.

Starting with emotions

Kick-off events normally begin with personal discussions intended to legitimize talking about one's concerns and ambitions. In all likelihood, the first personal conversations will not be very deep, but it is important to make a beginning. The only way to get people talking honestly is to get them talking, and show them that it is not only "safe" but also necessary to be honest in the discussions. The underlying message is "this is going to be different from what we talk about at the office."

Jan's objective was to achieve a gradual deepening and broadening of the dialog over the first few days, and to move away from the well-rehearsed debates that took place in the office. Each person would have to contribute personally – there was no sitting back and waiting for the CEO or finance director to give the usual PowerPoint presentation. The goal was to change the way the group and each individual looked at the challenges ahead, and to focus the emotional energy on moving forward rather than blocking progress.

We recommend that you start, as Jan did, with the "hopes and fears" exercise.

Exercise: hopes and fears

This exercise signals to participants that it is OK to talk about their feelings. Each person will bring to the MWB journey different levels of energy and enthusiasm. Some will embark on the journey saying "this process is exactly what we need at this point in time"; others will be sure that it will be a complete waste of time. Still others will have personal agendas that they hope they can further, perhaps scoring wins for their areas of the business, or for their credibility in the eyes of the leader. The hopes and fears discussion starts to tease some of these barriers and agendas into the open where they can be discussed and, if necessary, defused.

The exercise begins in a very focused way, with each group member asked to discuss her or his hopes and fears with respect to how the MWB event, and the whole journey, might unfold and what it might yield. Then, with probing, the conversation can usually be broadened into a more general discussion of everyone's hopes and fears for themselves, the management group, and the future of the business.

If some people are reluctant to engage, our advice to the leader at this point is: "Don't push it." Let people be as open or closed as they wish. Some people will naturally take longer to feel comfortable with this type of discussion, and there is nothing to be gained by trying to push them into it right off the bat. Peer pressure will work wonders as the week goes on.

The leader should also be able to use this opening exercise to set expectations. Through responses to the comments and questions of others, it is usually possible to indicate what is and is not possible with an MWB process. The journey is not, for example, a quick fix; nor is the kick-off event a love-in which will leave everyone feeling good but the business no further advanced. Some tough choices will have to be made and there are likely to be periods of stress and disagreement. These and similar messages can be delivered in a matter-of-fact way as responses to the hopes and fears of the group as they arise.

Exercise: myths and taboos

The "myths and taboos" exercise flows naturally from the hopes and fears discussion. A myth is an unconscious, taken-for-granted "truth" that the group never questions, but should. A taboo, on the other hand, is something that everyone in the group knows but does not discuss.

The aim of the exercise is to uncover both myths and taboos, to encourage more open conversation, and remove barriers that could stop the group moving forward effectively.

At first glance, many myths appear to be completely rational "facts," but on closer examination they turn out to be driven more by emotion – by collective hopes and fears, for example – than reality. Here are a few examples we have heard debated by management teams.

Typical industry-related myths

- Ours is a no-growth, unattractive industry, which is why our financial performance is poor. (This myth conveniently ignored the fact that several competitors were performing far better.)

- You have to be big and global to perform well in this industry, so unless we can make an acquisition, we will not be able to improve our performance. (There were clear exceptions to this "rule" about being big and global that many participants preferred to overlook.)

- The products being produced by Chinese competitors are clearly inferior, and will never be purchased by Western customers. (For how long?)

Typical company-related myths

- Our products are superior to those of the competition. (The best way to test this is to ask whether this superiority results in a price premium being charged, or strong gains in market share.)

- We should never compete directly with company X. They are too good. (Often such statements are based on single incidents that took place a decade ago.)

Typical myths about the organization

- We have strongly shared values and a strong culture. (This may mean nothing more than everyone carries the wallet card with the company values on it. It seldom means anything about the actual behavior of executives.)

- We are customer focused. (This is easy to say, but needs to be supported by solid evidence.)

● Different parts of the organization work well together when the chips are down. (Jan's group had many examples to the contrary.)

It is easy to see how such myths, if widely held and never surfaced, can influence how a management team sees its capabilities, its competitors, and its options for the future. In fact, if left untested the myths can unnecessarily constrain conversations and possibly lead teams to false conclusions about what are, or are not, their MWBs. This is why it is important to get them on the table early in the MWB journey. One advantage of including a few younger managers in your MWB kick-off event, as mentioned in the last chapter, is that they do not know (or believe) all of the myths.

The discussion of the company's myths took Jan's group much longer than expected, as every proposed myth was hotly debated, with half the team arguing, "that is not a myth, that is true." Here's what they came up with:

Our myths (things held as absolute truths in the organization)

● We are:
  – efficient, successful, humane, externally focused, world class
  – a strong team with a strong culture
  – in a tough industry, with big barriers to growth.

● We will:
  – continue to be successful because we know the customers best
  – solve problems if we are allowed – be great if THEY don't stop us.

● Our work practices are "smart":
  – all problems can be solved with a process
  – all our processes are good – and not bureaucratic.

● Our decisions:
  – are based on value-added for the company
  – emphasize that we have little to learn from others.

The debate about myths often leads directly to a discussion of taboos, as the two are closely related. Jan's group came up with quite a lot:

Our taboos (things that cannot be openly discussed or addressed in the organization)

● Addressing under-performance.

● Openly disagreeing with plans and targets.

● Suggesting competitors are as good as or better than us.

- Challenging intuition/feelings that are presented as data.
- Rebalancing resources significantly.
- Stopping projects/initiatives.
- Holding managers accountable.
- Saying cut the crap, get on with it.
- Talking about personal failure.

This is probably the first session where the "fish" are going to land hard on the table, and it is almost guaranteed to be uncomfortable. Why do something that is sure to cause discomfort? As we said earlier, unless you can talk about reality – the real issues – there is no use embarking on an MWB journey. The challenge is to avoid being unremittingly negative or overly optimistic – back to Jim Collins: "Confront the brutal facts (yet never lose faith)."[1]

Given these facts will often involve the leader, it is essential that she or he not become defensive or punish whoever dares to speak the truth. Let the fish land and discuss them. The list about the CEO could be a long one. Here are some common examples:

- The CEO avoids confrontation.
- The CEO relies too much on executive X, who has a strong set of biases that distort our decisions.
- The CEO makes too many decisions on his/her own.
- When it comes to bad news, the CEO is likely to "shoot the messenger," with the result that bad news is not delivered upward in a timely fashion.

Because a lot of myths and taboos relate directly to the organization's culture and how its people interact, this is often a good point to move the group on to a discussion of how they operate as a team.

Exercise: how do we operate as a team?

The point of this exercise is to hold up a mirror to the group and have them think and talk beyond their self-imposed barriers (including the myths and taboos just discussed), and about how they operate in different situations, including how they handle conflict. The point of

[1] Collins, Jim (2001) *Good to Great*, Random House Business Books, UK.

the debate is to be realistic about what works and what doesn't in terms of how they operate – to face up to the fact that the THEY in the myth "solve problems if we are allowed – be great if THEY don't stop us" is actually WE.

The topics you cover will depend on the issues the leader and group have surfaced prior to and during the event so far, but you may find it useful to go back to the characteristics of the high-performing teams that we described in Chapter 2 and ask:

Do we work well together?

● Does the team accept the leader?

● Does the team communicate honestly and openly?

● Does each individual feel personally committed to the team agenda, and does their individual agenda support that of the team?

● Do the managers respect one another?

● Does the team handle conflict effectively?

● Once a decision is made, does everyone support it?

● Does the team have legitimacy in the eyes of others?

● Do team members feel mutually accountable for results?

Again these debates will bring out some important "home truths," as Jan's team found out when they discussed how they handled conflict:

In our team, conflict is . . .

● Not welcomed, viewed as bad for your career.

● Personalized.

● Driven by consensus toward the lowest common denominator.

● Ignored, avoided, delegated, or resolved slowly.

● Not seen as constructive.

● Managed as part of the annual plan discussion.

● Dealt with outside the room.

● Tackled by throwing money at consultants.

● Resolved by individual lobbies, vested interests, compromise.

● Avoided by debating endlessly.

● Dissipated in lengthy discussion.

● Considered anti-team and destructive.

Facing these realities also enables the group to realize what they look like to the people below and around them in the organization, and that may not be a pretty picture. The myths, taboos, and "modus operandi" of the group have a strong influence on how the rest of the organization operates. What is dysfunctional at the top can be magnified hugely across an organization, with significant impairment of overall performance.

The myths and taboos debate sparked an emotional crisis between three members of Jan's team. Jan himself then became upset, and wanted to get away from the issue that was causing the problem and retreat to safer ground. But with a major effort he restrained himself and let the debate take its course. Ultimately the situation was resolved after several private interventions by the facilitator.

Flashpoint! Restructuring versus growth

One team from a large multinational started their MWB journey in the midst of a major restructuring exercise. The leader of the team (which included forty executives from across geographies and functions) had a clear objective in mind for the event – the team had become too focused on the short-term restructuring and were starting to make decisions that would have a negative long-term impact on the business. The business was getting into the mode of across-the-board cuts, significant ones at that. The leader felt strongly that the restructuring process needed to balance improving short-term performance and laying the foundation for the years ahead.

In the first stage of the kick-off event, the team directly challenged the leader, with many executives speaking out strongly: "Why are we wasting our time here? We all know what we need to do and that is restructure the business." "You are not being honest with us. You already know the target cuts and you are just trying to take us to an answer you already know." The comments just kept coming, with increasing levels of passion. The frustration that had been building in the organization was exploding right in front of the leader, now in the awkward position of having to respond on the spot.

The event was halted temporarily to allow a frank exchange of views. Executives voiced their frustrations and the leader listened and honestly addressed many of the concerns that were raised. "Yes, we are in a period of crisis, but our role as leaders (of an organization of 20,000-plus

▶

employees) is not just to cut jobs and shut down plants. Our role as leaders is to build a sustainable long-term business proposition." After an hour and a half, it was agreed that one sub-team would explicitly address the restructuring issues; all the other teams would provide input to this team. The rest of the teams would then carry on with the agenda as agreed. Each team had an hour to discuss and provide input.

The clash, although sharp, was clearly the turning point in the event. The leader listened, responded, and built the trust of the team. At the end of the event, the team gave the leader a standing ovation, with most expressing the opinion that how he had handled the crisis demonstrated his commitment to the team and the future of the business. It was an important step in building a new level of trust and setting new rules for how the team would work together, in good times and in bad.

Exercise: personal lifeline

The personal lifeline exercise is usually done at the end of the first day of a kick-off event. The day has already been charged with a lot of emotional energy – it's about to get even more personal. The objective is simple: if we are going to work together more effectively than before, we need to know more about each other as people and start to foster personal relationships and trust. (Remember, this is a big hurdle for the collection of individuals who typically make up a management team – see Chapter 3.)

How does it work? Earlier in the day, everyone is asked to reflect on their lives. What have been the high points and what have been the lows? What have been defining events in their life? How do they see themselves as people, what matters most to them, what do they want the people around them to know that may currently be hidden? Each individual will then share their experiences and thoughts with a small group, usually only three or four people in total to promote the sense of intimacy and privacy that is absolutely necessary for any meaningful dialog. It is purely verbal, nothing is written down. The role of the group is to listen and support each speaker, asking questions as needed for clarification, but not challenging. In the briefing for the exercise, emphasis is placed on how questions should be asked, with suggested non-threatening formats, for example "tell me more" or "what made you think that?" Again, the aim is understanding, not criticizing.

Clearly, some people will find this exercise uncomfortable. In fact, some will reject it outright and refuse to participate, although this is rare and what normally happens is that the person stays on the "surface," confining their thoughts to "safe" topics. Others will delve far deeper, sharing much more, and in many cases discovering more about themselves through the conversations.[2] Often, it will be the leader who shows the way. While the rest of the group splits into small groups for this part of the day, the leader normally does his personal lifeline first, in front of the whole group. This can be daunting, but it is important to demonstrate that what he is asking of his team, he is prepared to do himself – modeling the transparency and trust he hopes they can build together.

This exercise is often a defining moment for the group and marks a significant change in the style of interactions. There is still a long way to go in building deeper relationships and openness, but the door has now been opened for these new behaviors.

An alternative format for this exercise is based on the appreciative inquiry (AI) approach.[3] The team divide into pairs and interview each other for forty-five minutes, again in a comfortable and private environment. The aim is to allow each person in turn to tell their story, using a set of questions to prompt for more detail on topics including core values, career choice and working experiences, leadership experiences, and personal change and transition. In line with the AI philosophy, questions are worded to focus on "positive potential," that is, to build constructive conversations that foster energy and imagination and look toward future opportunities.

[2] A note for those interested in the background theory: if you think about this in terms of the widely used Johari Window concept (first published in a working paper at the University of California Western Training Laboratory in 1955 by Joseph Luft and Harrington V. Ingham; see Luft, J. (1970), Group Processes, An Introduction to Group Dynamics, 2nd edition, National Press Books, Palo Alto, CA, USA), the exercise reveals things known to you but not to others ("hidden") and potentially things known to others but not known to yourself ("blind").

[3] The appreciative inquiry theory was initially developed in 1986 by David L. Cooperrider in an unpublished doctoral dissertation at Case Western Reserve University, Cleveland, Ohio; then published in 1987 in "Appreciative Inquiry in Organizational Life," D. L. Cooperrider and S. Srivastva, in Pasmore, W. and Woodman, R, (eds) *Research in Organization Change and Development*, Vol. 1, JAI Press, Greenwich, CT. Since then there have been many articles and studies published that have elaborated the ideas and applications – please see *http://appreciativeinquiry.cwru.edu/* for further information and resources.

Whichever approach you choose, the conversations help to create energy, openness and ideas that can be linked to the change agenda that is being developed during the MWB journey.

Broadening intellectual horizons

The energy that has been created by the initial exercises can now be put to work on the "intellectual" strategy challenges. The idea here is to move the discussion to the level of the company and marketplace (from individual and team levels) and to look at the "same old" strategy inputs in different ways. The team will not be doing "traditional" strategic analysis – hopefully most of the inputs for these discussions (market segmentation, customer analysis, competitor profiles, and so on) will already be pasted up on the walls around them. Rather they will be directly experiencing and applying this strategic "database" to generate and align deeper insights about where they think the business really is today, what are the most significant challenges it faces, and what it could potentially achieve in the future.

Several exercises are particularly useful for this and provide the "raw material" to start thinking in earnest about MWBs. (For a roadmap reference, go back to Figure 4.2: you will see that we are moving from the personal lifeline activity to the "business lifeline" exercise.) Normally we start this part of the event with a "test" of how the different team members see the history of the business: the business lifeline.

Exercise: business lifeline (inside-out)

The business lifeline has some similarities with the personal lifeline. Again the team will be looking back over time – how much depends on the tenure of the team, but generally at least three or four years – and thinking about the highs and lows, this time for the business. A large piece of paper is the centerpiece and each person plots along the timeline the highs and lows from their perspective, against a common set of agreed events such as product launches, acquisitions, or major organizational changes.

Although the events are common, the perspectives on the success and failure of each will invariably not be. Because each person has a different view from his or her area of the organization, perspectives can be dramatically different – we regularly see big differences in views across countries and between business units and the center. Take, for example:

- The launch of a major new product across all markets for a leading snack foods producer.
    - HQ's view: it is a major success in building a common brand and production infrastructure, and has great associated cost efficiencies.
    - Country's view: HQ is taking away our local products that consumers identify with and asking us to execute on products that are totally untested here – "we've slogged away to reach the number one position; why are they undoing all our good work?"

- The shut-down of a production plant after a rationalization of the European product portfolio of a global foods company.
    - Country A (losing plant): it's a nightmare trying to manage the redundancy program, regulations mean it will cost us more than running it as a back-up plant for two years, by which time we think volumes will be up enough to make it viable again; it's going to hurt sales too because local government and customer perceptions of our commitment to the country are at rock bottom.
    - Country B (plant with consolidated volumes): at last we have realistic capacity utilization potential; we can make investments and really work toward greater efficiencies; the workforce are delighted that they have security after a period of huge uncertainty.
    - HQ: it makes sense to use our capacity most efficiently in this way and we should save costs as a result, while delivering higher-quality products.

- The move from a country-based organization to a category-based organization for the European division of a US multinational, which involved job changes (including some job losses) for many of the European senior team.
    - HQ US: it makes things a lot more streamlined and reflects the reality of our markets which are increasingly cross-border in Europe with the introduction of the euro; it also aligns much better with how we organize here in the US so makes reporting lines and core processes such as strategy and new product development much more transparent and integrated.
    - European CEO: from a market perspective I can see the rationale, but my team is in complete disarray – there is in-fighting for the

new category head positions and I know my star country head in Italy is going to leave; he's a fantastic innovator, but would never move from his home country to the European HQ. We have to get it sorted out fast or our key competitor will take advantage.

- Country A managing director: who is going to deal with the local regulators and make sure the voice of the local consumer is heard? I'm going to go for the category head position because if not I just don't know what my role is going to be – I'll probably be demoted if not and have no way to get things done.
- New category head designate: rationalizing the supply chain is what we have needed to do for a long time and I think the new European approach will be a great success, but we have to figure out how we customize for local demand, and the guys on the ground in the countries are not cooperating right now.

The value of this exercise is in surfacing these different perspectives on where the company has been as an organization, so the team can start to build a common interpretation. The opportunity to explain *why* the perspectives are different on the same events is critical. Understanding how others around you see the same events is the basis for forging a new way of communicating, as well as seeing challenges from different angles which can spark new ideas and options for the future. Again, it sets the foundation for taking a collective view of the choices and trade-offs that defining MWBs will require.

Exercise: outside-in perspectives

Now it's time to actively break down traditional, internally focused perspectives. The executives in the room are still using the data on the walls to look at their situation – but now from the outside-in. The exercises involve a series of role-play dialogs where the executives take the perspective of a series of stakeholders. The stakeholders used in the exercises can vary, but the exercises are designed to provide a critical input into identifying MWBs through a rigorous assessment of the likely future intentions and/or moves of the key stakeholders in your environment. The group will naturally think first of investors, competitors and key customers, but there could be other players such as regulators, suppliers, unions, or non-governmental organizations such as Greenpeace, any of which might play an important role in their future success.

The idea is to confront the team with the views of these various stakeholders in full and unabridged "technicolor." We ask them to place themselves in the shoes of investors, financial analysts, customers and/or consumers, and competitors, then to take a long hard look at the company. What do they see, what are their views of its strengths and weaknesses, where do they see the challenges, and what do they want from the company?

The point of the exercises at this stage is to build on the data and insights you already have, both on the walls and in the heads of the team. You want to give meaning to it through the dialogs and role-plays, so you can interpret the implications for the company – and hence for the choices you will need to make as you determine your MWBs.

However, moving away from internal perspectives can be alien because the team is so entrenched in its own view of the world. How many management teams really listen to the "raw" feedback from their environment or seize opportunities from it? (See box below.) Less than you would think – often the information is heavily filtered before it reaches the desks of executives or sometimes it is outright ignored. So the leader or facilitator will need to provide a source of challenge, at least early on until the team gets really engaged, which is typically the case because it can be liberating to be the "outsider."

Taking opportunities from consumer feedback

One large media company had dozens of feedback lines ready to take calls from its audiences – from providing gardening fact sheets, radio schedules, and advice on information sources for health issues to fielding complaints.

It was a costly part of the operation, but no one in the executive team ever saw the feedback. They simply did not know that hundreds of people had been outraged by a controversial program on genetic engineering, or that hundreds more had loved the coverage of a major national event, at least until other parts of the media picked up on such stories (usually negative ones). Moreover, the staff who had made the programs felt like they were operating in a vacuum. Even if they did generate real public interest (and the staff could check the feedback if they wanted to), no one in authority ever offered praise or advice on how to deal with any fall-out.

▶

> When the executive team finally revamped their performance measures and started looking at the audience feedback, some in "raw" quotes, they found a huge number of ideas for improvements – some very simple and small, but many of which would have a significant positive impact on audience perceptions.

Below are some examples of how the exercises can unfold.

Investor/analyst perspective

A mid-sized media company had a core, predominantly offline (print-based) business which generated significant amounts of cash (the "cash cow"[4]). As multimedia opportunities (and competitors) proliferated, particularly online, management was increasingly starting to focus on and talk publicly about a multimedia strategy, moving from print to web-based products and eventually becoming a full-service media company. What did external people with an interest in the company think?

First, the team took the analyst perspective. They debated: is the company an attractive investment? On the plus side, analysts saw profitability, strong cash flow, and a dominant market position, reinforced by a leading brand. Conversely, growth was negative, the customer base was high risk, costs were a worry, and strategy was far from clear, with product development being very short-term focused. To move from a "hold" to a "buy" rating, the company would need to invest in its core business, rebalance its channel/product portfolio, cut costs, and create clear value that would retain and build its customer base. Overall, the analyst perspective suggested huge potential that would not be too difficult to realize – but was management too complacent to do so?

With that question hanging in the air, it was time to take the investor view. Here, they asked: is the industry attractive? What makes a firm attractive? While investors saw an industry that had attractive high and

---

[4] This term refers to a quadrant on the "growth-share matrix" developed by the Boston Consulting Group (*www.bcg.com*) and denotes a business that is low growth but generates high amounts of cash relative to other businesses within the portfolio being reviewed.

sustainable margins, they were concerned about its future. The key
players, including the media company, were seen as confused, lacking
clear direction, and with potentially unproven future business models.
The term that was most worrying for the team was "turnaround
potential." Added to this, they recognized that investors were not all
alike – yield investors were looking for a stream of (preferably
increasing) dividends versus the growth investors who were less risk
averse, while the private equity buyers were on the look-out for
turnaround opportunities. The messages from the analyst perspective
were reinforced: the core business needed to be secured and healthy
while new online models were developed. Strategic clarity and internal
efficiencies would also be critical if they were to attract the types of
investors they wanted rather than deserved.

Customer/consumer perspective

So what did the customers who paid for their services think about their
strengths and weaknesses? What did the company need to do to be a
preferred supplier? Here, the team referred to the customer feedback
information pasted on the wall, as well as their own experiences. This
echoed the analysts' worry that the customer base was not secure by
any means. Yes, they were an industry leader with good products and
returns for customers. But they were falling into traps associated with
monopolists and large, bureaucratic companies. Service was great when
things went right, but arrogant and slow when they didn't.
Communication was not clear, prices were hiked without good
rationales, and administration was complex, particularly for the larger
customers. Again, the message was, get the basics right, make sure the
cash cow is delivering above and beyond customer expectations. And
focus externally to provide customer value – build a culture centered
on helping the customer and simplifying annoying bureaucracy.

The fourth and final perspective that the team took was that of the user,
the people who used their services to find information about the
customers, paying for some but not all channels. The company was
seen as a trustworthy institution, generally accessible and easy to use.
But the lack of customer/consumer focus was again evident: services
were not always user friendly, in fact some were distinctly hostile, and
perceived to be expensive. Inconsistencies in information between
channels highlighted the internal silo mode of operation within the

company. To be the preferred supplier, they would have to simplify and really understand user needs better to deliver improved services.

The group looked at each other silently as they finished discussing the final perspectives. It was clear that they had a lot to do and they needed to start looking externally fast if they were to maintain their leading position. The core business had to be secured as a priority and they had to start listening much better and responding to market needs – they had lost touch.

In this example, the messages from the various stakeholders were consistent. This is not always the case. Sometimes, different groups want very different things from a company. Tough choices will need to be made about whose needs to prioritize as MWBs are defined.

Hearts and minds of competitors

A further outside-in perspective that teams often take is that of competitors. In the "hearts and minds" exercises the leader asks sub-groups within the team to role-play key external players. To make the role-plays as realistic as possible, each group is provided with information on both the organization in question and, to the extent possible, the personalities of its management team. (In order to collect the appropriate information, you need to think about the possible role-plays in advance of the kick-off event.) In some cases we have assigned groups to role-play particular competitors or customers as necessary throughout the remainder of the week. So if the group needs to gauge a competitive reaction to a variety of proposed moves, it can be done relatively quickly. And this is the central purpose of the "hearts and minds" exercise – we want to move beyond static analysis and get into the dynamics of the situation. If we do X, how will key external actors respond? Then how will we react to their move? And so on.

The power of the hearts and minds exercises is that they bring to life organizations other than your own. Typically managers enjoy playing the role of a major competitor (or a difficult customer) or maybe an important new entrant who is carrying no historical baggage. It can be liberating and fun. But the results can be sobering.

Imprinted deeply on our memory is the session in which a sub-group of managers was asked to play an aggressive competitor and created an innovative and devastating response to the original group's plan. Then the session became acrimonious, with comments coming from the main group such as, "that's not fair – they would never do that – the only reason you thought of that is because you know our thinking." Unfortunately the company proceeded as planned, as if the role-play had never taken place, and the competitor in question reacted exactly as the role-playing managers had predicted. The result was an expensive disaster.

For Jan's group this exercise was fun, and although they went into it expecting to discover nothing new, as they had been through strategy reviews many times, they were surprised when the group playing a non-government organization (NGO) surfaced several issues that no one had taken seriously before. This group's role-play was so convincing that it was decided the team needed to learn more, quickly. It was arranged that a staff specialist (who until this point had been ignored in all strategic discussions) would join the group the following day to make a presentation on the NGO in question.

Building alignment on a future ambition

The most compelling MWBs are externally focused. Why? Because this is where the future success of the company lies. Even if the team has been chastened by looking at their challenges through someone else's eyes, figuring out how to serve a customer better than your competitors should excite more passion and creativity than debating internal issues such as transfer prices. If not, you have a problem!

the most compelling MWBs are externally focused

After some solid grounding in the intellectual "database," it is now time to encourage the team to apply the insights as they look to the future of the company. Earlier we described strategy as involving "informed choices and timely actions." To make collective choices, there must first be some agreement on the shared ambition of the group. Without such agreement, executives could end up making unilateral choices about moving to different futures, or trying to achieve different objectives.

A key challenge we have found in making choices about a shared future direction is balancing the trade-off between being too incremental and limited by current activities to envision a future, and being so long-term focused that any discussion is about dreams. Figures 4.3 and 4.4 present a sharp comparison between a future goal-oriented approach such as "looking back" and a more traditional incremental approach.

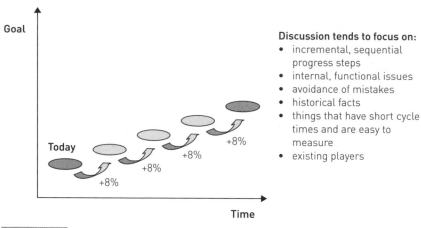

Discussion tends to focus on:
- incremental, sequential progress steps
- internal, functional issues
- avoidance of mistakes
- historical facts
- things that have short cycle times and are easy to measure
- existing players

Figure 4.3 Typical short-term growth planning process

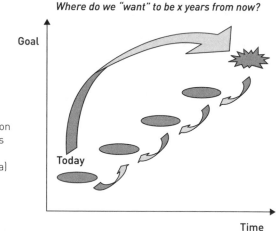

Where do we "want" to be x years from now?

Discussion tends to focus on:
- external environmental factors
- undefined, non-linear progress steps
- business as a whole (not functions)
- learning and experimentation
- multiple options and results
- things that are tough to measure (by traditional data)
- long cycle times
- potential for new players and roles

Figure 4.4 Growth destination planning process

In the exercise we describe here, there is a mix of both intellectual and emotional input: the team need to think about concrete issues and opportunities realistically, but now is the time to really start to stir up excitement and build a shared aspiration for the future.

Exercise: looking back on our success (inside-out)

Now that the group has a shared sense of how its competitive marketplace might change in coming years, it is time to consider its longer-term aspirations. "Looking back on our success" is an exercise designed to do just that. It is about defining the whole vision for the company, beyond the "rational" strategy and budgeting goals, to include the look and feel of the organization. The exercise leads the group to talk about the legacy it wants to leave behind; how it wants its successors to see its contributions. The members discuss what this means in practice, not just in the abstract, considering such things as how they will identify and groom their successors, what explicit behaviors they need to adopt to encourage an open flow of ideas in the organization, and, perhaps, how a meritocracy will actually work.

The exercise begins with the leader explaining to the group that it is now five years in the future, and during that time everything has gone just as they had wanted it to. All targets have been met, and the organization is the one they wanted to create. So, the challenge to the group members is to identify their major aspirations for the business on two dimensions: (1) what do they want to achieve? And (2) what do they want to become?

If important disagreements arise during these discussions, you must spend the time to reach a resolution, because if the group does not agree on where it wants to take the business, the rest of its conversations will be futile. For example, we recently worked with a management group in which half the members saw growth as the top priority over the coming five years, whereas the other half believed that the first priority had to be significantly improving profitability, and only then should growth be the focus. Left unresolved, such a fundamental disagreement was going to hang over all subsequent discussions, so the leader insisted that the group take the time to explore the disagreement in more depth and reach a resolution: which it did.

Because the "looking back on our success" exercise is broad and open-ended, unexpected ideas can emerge. Do not kill them – they could be important. It is also important that the leader does not insist on his or her vision of the future. We recently did this exercise with a team which already had an agreed five-year plan in place, driven largely by the CEO. Initially, they just "went through the motions," playing back to us what had already been decided. However, as they discussed the characteristics of the organization that they wanted to have in five years, one manager said the real key to creating the desired organizational culture was to take the company public. The group had previously discussed an IPO several times, but had always decided that the timing was not right. Suddenly, however, the pace and intensity of the discussion increased dramatically and in the end, the group concluded that an IPO within the next two to three years could be the key to creating the future they wanted for themselves and the organization. That conclusion impacted all remaining debates in the kick-off event.

Finishing the "opening windows" part of the event on a high note as the group thinks about what possibilities the future holds is important. Opening windows is typically a roller-coaster ride. The energy and excitement created by a compelling vision will fortify the team for the demanding debates and choices that are part of defining their MWBs.

Jan had initially been skeptical of the value of spending much time on the "looking back" exercise. And indeed in the end the group's portrait of the desired future was not very far from where he had thought it should be, before the discussion began. But he was amazed at some of the debates along the way. Things that Jan thought obvious appeared to be new ideas to some members of the team, and he had to bite his tongue not to intervene to cut off debates that he regarded as a waste of time. But as he came to realize later, these debates were vital to the people involved. The envisaged organization of the future, with its culture of winning, became more than just an intellectual idea: it became a real place where people actually wanted to work. The debates had engaged the "whole" person, not just the rational brain, and the result was a strong emotional commitment to a new future.

It had been an illuminating day and a half, all told, he thought as he joined the group on the way to lunch. He had not heard this much lively conversation between them since he had started. The question was, could they turn the energy that seemed to have started bubbling through into something concrete?

5
five

Defining the battles: colliding to decide

As he entered the breakfast room on the morning of day three, Jan sensed that the preparation for the day's debates on the MWB list had already begun. Maria, in charge of sales, and Jack, who ran marketing, were huddled over cups of coffee, talking intently. As he walked over to join them, he heard a snatch of the conversation: "But it's got to be the top priority. It's going to spread and hit us hard in the Netherlands soon. I just don't know how Boris will take it." Jan knew his somewhat mercurial head of R&D did not always see eye to eye with the customer-facing directors, and Maria's comment reinforced his feeling that the upcoming sessions would be challenging; he just hoped they would also be productive.

★ ★ ★

Colliding to decide

What do we mean by colliding to decide? It conjures up (politically incorrect) visions of banging heads together to get agreement on a critical issue or maybe (slightly less politically incorrect) shutting people in a small (uncomfortable) room until they reach a consensus on an important decision (à la a papal conclave). We don't advocate going this far in an MWB event, but the principles still apply: this part of the process is about making choices, tough choices in many cases. The key is to make sure these choices are both fully informed and robustly challenged before final agreement is reached.

Why collide to decide?

In Chapter 4 we described the challenge of opening windows as putting important issues – including the often unspoken ones – on the table and moving executives beyond discussing data to building shared insights about the business and the organization. Now the focus moves from developing insights to making collective choices that will drive decision making, resource allocation, and management attention in the months and years to come. Strategy is about choice and now is the time to make the choices. But the choices must not be made by a leader acting in isolation or by asking individuals to make presentations on their pieces of the pie, hoping that they will fit together. Colliding means fully and transparently engaging in the debate.

If you do it right, the collision process will allow you to tap into and take full advantage of the diversity of your team. Everyone's voice will be heard, and when you uncover serious differences of opinion, you need to address them, not ignore them. A healthy "collision" means that the differing perspectives in the room will influence both the choices that you evaluate and the decisions you make about those choices. You need to deal openly with differences of opinion because if you do not, the decisions you make will be resisted later as executives believe their views were not heard: "We didn't take that into account. I didn't have the opportunity to put forward our situation and thus I am not bound by the decision."

If you are the leader, don't forget the 75 percent rule. Recognize when to back off – you do not have all the answers. A decision that is made as the result of a collision of views will be a better decision, and will be better implemented than one you make alone.

The collision process

The opening windows exercises that the group has just finished – probably the previous day – should have been stimulating and interesting. Now the challenge is to take the insights and perspectives that you generated in those exercises and use them as a base for making collective choices. Making choices is more difficult, more intense, and usually not as much fun. The warm-up is over; you are now at the heart of the matter. So take as much time as you need to: in our experience the collision process can take anything from a couple of hours to a day and a half. The key is to ensure there is sufficient time for debate so that all issues and concerns are surfaced.

As we illustrate in Figure 5.1, the first step involves brainstorming, to turn your perspectives and insights into a long list of potential MWBs. Look at a number of alternatives, not only the safe options – be sure to push for some unconventional ideas. Then debate each of them. What are the advantages and disadvantages? What impact would each have on the overall business? What is the downside? Have you unearthed some new opportunities? What are the risks?

Next comes the hard part: using "reality checks" to whittle down the long list to the 3–5 MWBs that the team will collectively pursue. As a leader you will need to be very firm in the prioritization process. Remember the quote in Chapter 1: "Too many priorities mean no priorities." Do not be surprised if emotionally based disagreements erupt along the way. As we said earlier, debating the choice of MWBs may sound like an intellectual process, but it can be intensely emotional. If anyone's pet project or power base is threatened, they are going to react.

During the debates you need to keeping focusing the group on the common vision of the future that you defined during the "looking back on our success" exercise, for this shared goal is the most powerful tool that you have to hold the group together. Be sure to keep everyone looking forward – and at this point in the process you need to ensure that the debate is not about where you are going, but how you will get there.

The process suggested in Figure 5.1 is based on our experience, but you may wish to change the order and activities to suit your situation. One thing we do recommend strongly, however, is that you treat the selection of MWBs as an iterative process. Do not try to make final decisions about your MWBs the first time you list them. In the interests of space we have shown only three MWB iterations in Figure 5.1 – the first to create a long list, the second to settle on a preliminary shortlist, and the third to finalize this shortlist – but you might need more sessions before arriving at your final choices. Certainly, you will not get them in one shot. Do not push for closure too soon; you need to get as much buy-in as possible on the final list and that will take time.

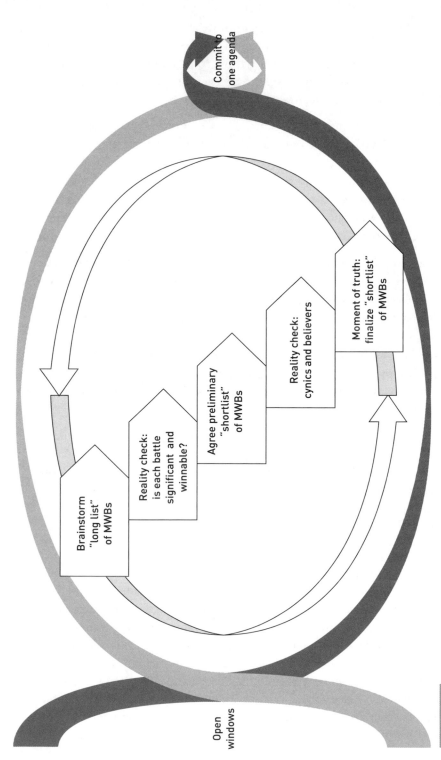

Figure 5.1 Colliding to decide

Brainstorm to create a long list

Even though your ultimate objective is to provide focus for your business by identifying only 3–5 key MWBs, we recommend you begin by casting a wider net and creating a longer list. In addition to the obvious benefit of having more alternatives to examine, making a longer list will allow you to avoid premature closure on what might be the favorite MWB choices of a couple of heavyweight players in your group. Looking at all the options also means listening to all the voices. So the long list is not just about getting more choices on the board, it is about getting more voices in the conversation. Do not let the impatience of the loud voices who already "know the answer" rush you to the shortlist.

As your discussion moves up and down the long list of MWBs, see whether you can combine some battles, refine others, and discard some. Try to restructure and refine each battle in such a way that you (a) maximize the impact the battle could have; (b) make the battle as externally focused as possible; (c) make it tangible and measurable; and (d) make it exciting. You will find that some of the battles will fail one or another of these tests and you can take them off the list immediately. These are battles that cannot hold their place even on the long list.

We outlined the criteria of a "good" MWB in Chapter 1, and we revisit the list here, as it is during the colliding to decide stage of the kick-off event that these factors really come into play.

Look for impact

A good MWB – if successful – will have a major impact on your business. Usually this means that in a multimarket or multiproduct business the impact of the MWB will reach across product and/or market boundaries. If you are considering an MWB that involves a push into a new country, for example, a country which offers growth opportunities for a number of your product lines will of course have much more impact than a country with a market for only one product line. The key point is to avoid limited-impact battles. Usually such battles are proposed only because they are the particular passion of individual managers who are looking to improve results in their part of the business or grow their local empires. Even on your long list, you need to ensure that each MWB is capable of making a major impact on your business.

Focus on external battles

Winning battles in the marketplace is what counts. This is how you create value. But when you first create your long list you are likely to find on it some battles that reflect long-standing internal debates about things such as transfer prices or internal territorial disputes about who can sell what where. Take such items off your list, and explain why. Get everyone focused on the battles that can increase the overall "size of the prize" – not on how you divide it up internally.

You may find, however, that your long list contains some battles that sound internal but can be reformulated to give them an external focus. For example, imagine that you have a problem delivering products on time in full to the appropriate quality standards. You could treat this as an internal battle, focused on your factories, or you could frame it as a customer-based issue and formulate the challenge in terms of winning market share or raising customer satisfaction levels in the relevant market segments. We strongly recommend the latter approach.

Take the browser wars of the late 1990s as another illustration of this approach. Bill Gates fired up the Microsoft team by making "beat Netscape" the MWB. Compare this to an internally focused interpretation: "develop and sell the most successful web browser." Of course, Microsoft's external battle required internal efforts and changes, but the way the organization engaged with the challenge could have been radically different if they had thought about it only in internal terms. You can see lots of potential for internal conflict: "it's the developer's fault," "it's the sales team's fault," "that's not what I mean by successful." With the simplicity and clarity of "beat Netscape," everyone knew that the test of what they did was against this shared goal, so energy was focused on realizing value in the marketplace, not on internal conflicts.

Once you have identified your key external battles you can establish the internal battles required to support the external battles and this is fair enough, but do not start with a lot of internal battles on your long list. If your team knows they are tackling an internal battle in order to win an external battle, the energy level is likely to be much higher.

Be tangible

As you re-examine and rework the items on your long list, do as much as you can to make each battle specific and tangible. We were nervous a couple of years ago when a group proposed "fuel for growth," as an MWB. It sounded hopelessly vague. However, with some effort, the battle was made specific and tangible. The challenge was redefined as freeing up $200 million to fund specific growth initiatives. Key sub-targets were put in place to generate specific amounts over each of the next three years, while reducing fixed assets. After the kick-off event a detailed benchmarking and best practice study was launched to quantify these targets further and determine precisely where the funds would be realized. By the end of the first year, this initiative was on track and the money was being put into the growth initiatives.

Make it exciting

You should try to include on your long list of MWBs at least a couple of battles that the organization – and the management team – would find really exciting. In Chapter 1 we distinguished between offensive and defensive MWBs and it is likely that offensive ones will create the most excitement. The reason we suggest you focus on excitement is that we have found that if MWBs are not exciting, the commitment and trade-offs required to win them are difficult to maintain over time. One executive stated: "The challenge is to frame the MWB so that it will create energy on a continuing basis, and people will be willing to make individual sacrifices as necessary, over the rest of the journey."

Consider the example of Carlsberg. Prior to 2000, the Carlsberg brand was losing ground. It had grown at only 1.6 percent per annum for the previous five years and market share was declining. But rather than devise MWBs about creating new brands or moving into non-beer beverages, the team addressed the problem head on and developed a battle that focused on expanding the Carlsberg brand. This was the company's heartland, and this was where the most energy and excitement resided. The long-term goal – challenging, to put it mildly – was to achieve double-digit growth. More focus was brought to bear on the brand in core markets, while in other markets it was repositioned, and there was increased investment in brand building. New energy soon spread across the company. Top-line growth accelerated markedly, and by 2003 the company was exceeding its targets. The financial benefit was substantial of course, but the impact was also felt in organizational terms, as everyone aligned in pursuit of a common goal, sharing ideas and marketing themes, materials, and so on. This well-chosen MWB proved capable of creating a huge amount of sustainable energy.

Reality check: is each battle significant and winnable?

You now have a long list of MWBs, and it is time for the central debate of the kick-off event to begin. The challenge is to reduce your long list into the right shortlist of MWBs. The battles on the shortlist are going to receive the lion's share of your resources in the months and maybe years ahead – so they had better be the right ones!

We suggest you cull the long list by using two reality checks. The first is a traditional, rational, intellectual assessment; the second is a more emotional check. To begin the intellectual process, take a hard look at each of the battles on the long list and ask the group to subject it to the key questions below. You may already have considered some of these questions, but revisit them, this time with full intensity.

1. Is this MWB of true importance in taking us to the future we want? What would happen if we ignored this battle, and chose not to fight it?

2. What would success in this battle look like after one year? After three years? How should we measure it?

3. Is this MWB winnable – either with today's organizational capabilities or with the addition of new capabilities we can develop in the time available?

4. What are the major obstacles we will have to address? What are the major risks we will have to manage? What would happen if we fought this battle and lost?

5. Who are the major stakeholders, in the organization and outside, that we will have to influence as we address this MWB? What are the concerns of each? How and when should we approach them?

The first two questions require that you return to the discussion about the potential impact of each MWB; this time you are looking for both a more detailed assessment of the potential impact of each battle and some real buy-in to that assessment. Thus if one executive is saying the whole future of the business hangs on a particular battle and others believe she or he is wildly overstating the case, dig in. Push for numbers and develop scenarios. Remember that just because only one person is arguing something different, it does not mean that she is wrong. Maybe she has more or different information to the others. As the debate goes on, you should find that impact assessments are becoming more specific.

As you assess what victory in each battle on the long list would mean in terms of impact on the business, make sure that you are not proposing to refight yesterday's battles rather than focus on tomorrow's. For example, a European company we know well was number two in its national market and had been fighting for years to catch up with the leader, a long-time rival. Most of its MWBs were about beating that rival. But now the industry was changing and national boundaries were disappearing: Europe was the relevant market of the future, not the national market. Very reluctantly management realized that the goal had to be survival in Europe, and the MWBs on the long list about becoming number one in the local market had to give way to a new MWB: finding a way to attract the attention of one of the big, fast-growing, European-wide players, and to form an advantageous alliance with them. This had not been the intention of anyone in the group when they had arrived for the kick-off event. Just in time, they began to focus on the future.

Exercise: assessing capabilities (can we win this battle?)

The impact assessment will probably have shortened your long list a little, or at least allowed you to rank the battles in terms of importance. Now turn your focus to whether or not the organization has the capabilities to win each of the battles on the long list, if taken alone. (We come back to the issue of whether they are winnable taken together later.) At this point the team needs to consider: if we embark on this battle, how will key competitors react? Are they strong enough to beat us? What capabilities will we need? Do we have them? If not, can we develop them in the time available, perhaps by forming a joint venture, licensing new technology, or re-examining the scope (or time frame) of the MWB. Maybe we do not need to act in all Asian markets simultaneously, for example, an early win in China would be good enough.

The key to addressing such questions is to think not just about your resources. If resources were all that mattered, large companies would always beat small ones. This is far from the truth, and the key thing to consider is what use you (and your competitors) can make of the resources you have. (This, by the way, is why we are not fans of "strengths and weaknesses" analysis, as such exercises tend to be static, and concentrate only on resources, not capabilities.) Our suggestion, illustrated in Figure 5.2, is that you consider both your resources and

Resources	X	Organizational characteristics	=	Organizational capability
• People • Financial capability • Technology • Physical assets • Market position • Reputation • etc.		• Way of working together • Performance measures for business and people • Way people are paid • Decision-making processes • Key aspects of culture • etc.		• Speed of response • Commitment to a course of action • Flexibility • Ability to grow quickly • Ability to work in foreign cultures • etc.

Figure 5.2 Assessing organizational capability

your key organizational features, to arrive at an assessment of your organizational capabilities – both current and future. And remember capabilities are relative – so the key is to assess your capabilities relative to those of your competitors. You may consider yourself strong, but they may be stronger.

The lists of items in Figure 5.2 are not intended to be exhaustive: they are just "thought starters" that we use to get management teams thinking beyond the resources list. We also emphasize the multiplication sign, which implies that your organizational characteristics can lead you to over- or under-perform, given what would be expected based on your resources. Some companies can, as the British say, "punch above their weight," while others never seem to perform as they should, given the resources at their disposal. The difference lies in their organizational capabilities.

The "aha" moment for Jan's team came as they considered the implications of Figure 5.2 and realized that they did not need new resources to win some of their MWBs. Back at the office, Jan had frequently been inundated with requests of "€10 million to do this and €5 million for that," but now the realization grew in the group that most of their problems lay in the way they worked together. They did not need more resources, they needed to make better use of the ones that they already had. This was a major change in the group's mind set, and for Jan, the best moment in the last two days.

Exercise: key stakeholder analysis

Another thing you should consider when thinking about your ability to win a MWB is the role that key stakeholders might play. Stakeholders are those people or bodies inside and outside the organization that have a stake in the outcome of the battles, whether as employees, unions, shareholders, customers, regulators, suppliers, and so on. The question is how each major stakeholder will react to each battle. Will they support it or try to derail it? What are their concerns? How, and when, do we need to address those concerns?

To frame such an assessment we suggest you use a chart like that presented in Figure 5.3, categorizing stakeholders as supporters of your battle, bystanders who will not impact the battle in one direction or the other, and resisters who will actively work against you.

Resisters	Bystanders	Supporters
High impact	High impact	High impact
Moderate impact	Moderate impact	Moderate impact
Low impact	Low impact	Low impact

Figure 5.3 Key stakeholder analysis

Within each category, distinguish between those groups that you expect to have a lot of impact, moderate impact, and low impact. Sometimes such an analysis can reveal unexpected allies – such as customer groups who would welcome the entry of a new supplier, or regulators who are trying to encourage more competition in a given sector. But equally the analysis might suddenly make you realize that powerful groups like Greenpeace may oppose you. When the analysis is complete, you have to decide how to gain the support of the potential allies you have identified, and how to neutralize or defeat the important resisters.

The reality check that you have just been through should allow you to rank your MWBs in terms of attractiveness and "winnability," as well as take some battles off your list. You may also have decided that some battles need to be delayed, as preliminary victories are required to clear the way for these later battles. Most groups also conclude that some of the battles on their long list are in fact mini-battles that are components of other battles. But in spite of all of this reshaping and repositioning, it is likely that your newly shortened long list will still be too long.

Agreeing on the preliminary shortlist of MWBs

Your objective now is to shorten the list to the 3–5 vital, winnable MWBs that will be critical if the group is to create the future that it wants. As you look at your proposed package of final MWBs it is time to consider what we call "interaction effects": while each battle may make sense on its own, the whole package may not. The most obvious question is whether or not the organization has the capabilities to win all of the battles that you are considering – if you are going to pursue them at the same time. Maybe each battle is winnable, but collectively the package is too much. So check that first.

As you are considering the capabilities issue, also put on one piece of paper the timing, impact and the probability of success of each battle. Figure 5.4 shows what the result might look like. This chart presents the level of capabilities required for each battle plotted against the time frame for delivering success. The size of the "bubble" indicates the level of impact expected from the battle, while the shading highlights the probability of success.

The beauty of this diagram is that it gives you a single picture that captures the key features of your MWB portfolio. And the measures for each battle do not have to be 100 percent accurate – at this stage of the process that is impossible anyway – the key is to see how the overall picture looks when you put all the battles together. Does it feel doable? Is it balanced? Will this portfolio really meet our needs? Are trade-offs going to have to be made – if so, where? Take for example the portfolio patterns in Figure 5.5 (overleaf), which would offer cause for concern.

If you have developed a portfolio that looks more like (a), (b), (c) or (d) in Figure 5.5 than the one in Figure 5.4, you should ask yourselves if this is really what you want. If, for example, you are following a highly aspirational medium-term vision, but all your MWBs are focused on not

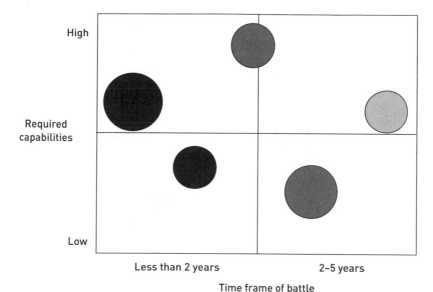

Note: MWBs with a very low probability of success (<30%) are unlikely to be chosen

Figure 5.4 Assessing your proposed MWB portfolio

disappointing analysts this year (pattern (a) in Figure 5.5), you are unlikely to reach your medium-term goals, so make sure your portfolio of MWBs is aligned with the business situation you face and the goals you are pursuing.

Once the team is happy that it has, broadly, a portfolio of MWBs that are aligned with its vision of the future, it is time to look at subtler interaction effects. These could include the impact of your MWBs on customers or competitors. Let's take a competitor who does not take you very seriously, for example. They might not be bothered much by the actions you will take to win one of your MWBs, but if you are suddenly moving in three areas at once, each of which impact on them, they might decide to devote significant resources to fight against you. In other words, you may have inadvertently wakened a sleeping giant.

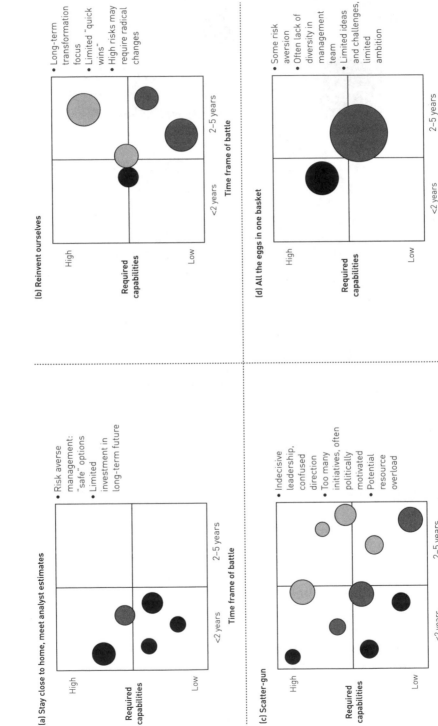

(a) Stay close to home, meet analyst estimates
- Risk averse management: "safe" options
- Limited investment in long-term future

(b) Reinvent ourselves
- Long-term transformation focus
- Limited "quick wins"
- High risks may require radical changes

(c) Scatter-gun
- Indecisive leadership, confused direction
- Too many initiatives, often politically motivated
- Potential resource overload

(d) All the eggs in one basket
- Some risk aversion
- Often lack of diversity in management team
- Limited ideas and challenges, limited ambition

Figure 5.5 MWB portfolio patterns that offer cause for concern

On the other hand, a customer might not be happy if you buy one of your competitors (who was also supplying that customer), dramatically increasing the customer's dependence on you, and at the same time enter into a joint venture that integrates you forward into your customer's business. Those moves might each make sense for you, but the combination may make your customer(s) feel threatened.

As we have said, every battle on the shortlist should have whole-hearted support from every member of the team. That may not be possible, at least at first, as the shortening process almost invariably creates winners and losers. Every item on the long list of MWBs will be "owned" by at least one member of the group, and thus every item cut means someone will perceive that they are losing. It is during this session that the group's emotional bonds, and the power of their future vision, will be put to the test. The key question is whether or not people are able to relate to the success of the group rather than just their individual interests. Hopefully, by this stage, the answer will be yes.

After much discussion and debate, Jan and his team created a shortlist of four MWBs. These were:

1. Fix the Belgian plant.

2. Create a new brand to fight Asian imports.

3. Introduce a premium product line in the UK.

4. Build Eastern Europe into 25 percent of the business within five years.

The most contentious item on the list was the first one. Everyone agreed that quality at the Belgian plant was poor and getting worse, but many argued that the problem was specific to one division and was not aspirational, and therefore should not be on the list. However, as the debate deepened it was pointed out forcefully that because the Belgian products were being sold under the same brand name as those of other divisions and were sold in related markets, it would be only a matter of time before consumer dissatisfaction (and associated declining market share) started to spread across divisions and borders. The issue was settled when Jan put his weight behind the choice. He did this because he truly believed the issue was immediate and vital, and he also suspected that the solution would involve cross-divisional cooperation, as two sister divisions would probably be able to help the Belgians solve their problem. Jan was deeply committed to doing everything he could to get the different parts of the company working together. He also liked the fact that the problem was potentially solvable in the near term. He thought that an early win would energize the whole MWB journey.

The second item on the MWB shortlist was much longer term in nature. In fact, one of the challenges facing the group in the second half of the week would be to put some dates and market share targets on this MWB. The idea of creating an "import fighter" brand had been debated in the company for some time but now, finally, it appeared that everyone was committed to doing it. It was recognized as a defensive move, as the new brand and products would probably never earn a lot of money because of their low margins. The main objective was to protect the traditional brand and product lines.

The UK had been suffering from increasingly strong own-label competition. Jan was convinced along with several others that they could no longer profitably fight the "low ground." They would need a more upmarket, premium brand positioned to attract consumers who were tired of supermarket labels. The debate around this had been going on since he had taken over. After looking at the issues from the perspectives of customers and competitors Jan was slightly less sure, but no one had really come up with an argument to kill it. Of the list of battles this was the one that everyone seemed least confident about.

The fourth MWB was the one that got the group excited. There was no doubt that everyone wanted to do it. There was clear agreement that this was where the exciting new growth opportunity was, an opportunity that would require focus and prioritization to build. There was agreement that within five years, these businesses needed to account for 25 percent of both revenue and profit. Right now, there was an important window of opportunity, one the company could not afford to miss. This battle was offensive, and offered an opportunity for real growth. The debating point was the capabilities issue. What new skills and knowledge would the company need to enter these new markets and successfully take on local competitors and other international firms who would also be rushing in? There was a feeling that they were already late, and some in the group were arguing for joint ventures or acquisitions as a way of engaging in this battle. This was an issue that would be discussed more fully in the second half of the week.

Apply reality check: cynics and believers

Once you have an agreed shortlist, it is tempting to sit back and say: "Done, let's get going." But as you can see from Jan's team above, there can be a lot of contentious debate about some of the battles chosen. It's time for a final reality check on this preliminary shortlist – this time an emotional one, because what you need is a committed team behind the chosen goals. Any lingering doubts need to be brought out into the open and dealt with, one way or the other.

Most management teams contain at least one cynic – many have several. These people and their predictably negative responses are often well known within the group. As one CEO put it, "Any cynic worth his salt is certainly going to be deeply skeptical about the MWB journey, the actual MWBs chosen, or anything else that starts with the management team going offsite for five days." Depending on the individuals, up to this point in the process the cynicism might be overt, or it might be hidden.

Exercise: cynics and believers

In either case, now is the time to make productive use of your cynics. An effective way to do this is to divide the management team into two and ask one half to be "believers" in each MWB on the shortlist, and the other to be cynics. Often it can help to "cast" people against type as it forces them to look at the issues through a new lens. The job of the cynics is to explain why each MWB is not important enough, or perhaps not aspirational enough, to be on the list. The believers, of course, have the opposite task. Halfway through we usually ask the cynics and believers to switch roles and argue the opposite point of view. Again, it helps them to switch lenses. Even more useful is to ask the teams how they feel now, perhaps as a lone voice against a choice. While the exercise is critical in decision making, it builds understanding and often empathy between team members who may not have understood each other's views well before.

The key in this exercise is to listen carefully to the cynical point of view – there is usually some valuable learning in it. During Jan's "cynics and believers" session, the cynics claimed that two items on the shortlist of MWBs were not really important, and were on the list solely because Jan thought they should be. No one else, the cynics claimed, believed in them. Furthermore, those MWBs would never be won, because once back at work, no one in the group would actually devote their best people to the tasks required to win the battles. After some initial hesitation, the rest of the group admitted that this was true. The result was a reopening of the debate about those two MWBs. Launching a premium brand in the UK disappeared from the list, while the group became convinced that fixing the Belgian plant was vital and pledged their support.

Moment of truth: finalize the shortlist

Now everyone has had a chance to speak. The battles on the shortlist have been subjected to rigorous testing. You have looked at each from many angles, thought about how you will overcome hurdles, and started forming a successful team in your mind. It is the "moment of truth" when the group needs to finalize the shortlist of MWBs that they will not only work on over the rest of the week at the event but champion over the course of the journey back at the office.

The last thing to do is to ask the "six million dollar question": what do we *really* think is the probability of success for the MWBs individually and collectively? Many teams hate this question. It is too soon to ask, they argue, and the question is unfair, as they are working with very preliminary information. They are right, but insist anyway. Make them do it. What is most interesting is not the probability of success per se, but the conditions they attach to it. You will hear things like, *if* R&D comes through with the new product in six months, *if* we can find a joint venture partner who knows the market, *if* a major customer will sign a development contract with us, and so on. These qualifying statements tell you where the real uncertainties and pressure points reside in the battle, and can already form a basis for planning the implementation of each battle.

The more the challenges that need to be addressed to win the MWBs are identified and shared during the process, the less room there will be for questioning the agenda once all return to the office. However, some participants may remain skeptical, arguing either that victory will not have as positive an impact as people are portraying, or that the MWB will be too difficult to win. Or, the group as a whole may conclude that they could win each battle separately, but the package of MWBs, taken together, is just too much. The management team may not have the collective will to engage in all of these battles: "We will stretch ourselves too thin."

In such a situation the goal should be to build an appetite for winning which will reinforce that collective will and drive the team to figure out how to overcome the inevitable barriers on the road to success. Focus on the power of victory, not the constraints. However, if you agree with the naysayers, you will need to reconsider either the battles or the composition of your management team.

the goal should be to build an appetite for winning

Jan's team protested as expected, but as they assessed the size of the prizes and the probabilities of winning, they confirmed their shortlist of three MWBs:

1. Fix the Belgian plant.
2. Create a new brand to fight Asian imports.
3. Build Eastern Europe into 25 percent of the business within five years.

Predictably, there were some "ifs" about whether R&D would come through on the new brand, and how many markets they would have the resources to move into simultaneously in Eastern Europe.

It had been a good but exhausting three days Jan thought as he collapsed into bed on Wednesday night. He was not quite sure what the group was thinking, but he suspected that a few were fully committed to what was going on, and even the skeptics were reserving judgment, waiting to see what tomorrow would bring.

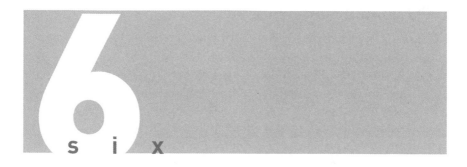

Breaking the silos: committing to one agenda

Jan awoke with a start. He had not slept well as the tense moments of the previous day's debates had been cycling through his mind all night. The first thing he saw as his feet hit the floor was the handwritten MWBs list that he had stuck on the wall the previous evening. As he looked at the list he felt a growing fear that, in spite of the emotion involved in the process, the shortlist of MWBs would remain just that – a nice list. Nothing would happen; nothing would change.

In the past Jan had often seen the same managers agree and make commitments during meetings only to fall back into disagreements, conflict and inaction afterwards. He was particularly worried about the simmering tension between Boris (R&D) and Maria (sales). Most of the time they kept things under wraps, but he had seen some open warfare in the final selection of the MWBs the previous day, and he was sure there was more to come.

As he prepared to meet with the group to begin the final two days, Jan wondered what he could do while they were still together in the mountains to make the MWBs become a continuing focus for action after the return to the office. The business clearly needed change, and he suspected that failure to achieve any meaningful results from the MWB process could also impact on his own career prospects. Not a happy thought, as he headed downstairs for breakfast.

Why commit to one agenda?

The MWB list is now ready. You have made progress. But Jan is right, there is important work still to be done. If everyone were to return to work now, the MWBs would probably be implemented half-heartedly, if at all, and could soon disappear from the management agenda. Before the kick-off event ends, he needs to make sure that the MWB agenda is fully understood and owned by the whole team so that once back at the office they will start behaving in a new and different way: working as a team – with one common, overriding agenda.

In Chapter 4 we explained how the opening windows process allows you to move your team from talking about data and analysis to building shared insights and perspectives. In Chapter 5 the focus was on moving from these shared insights to making collective choices that reflect the ambitions and vision of the whole group – not just those of individuals. Now you are in the final phase of the kick-off event and the goal is to make sure that everyone understands the implications of the MWB choices, both for the team as a whole and for each individual member of the team. Everybody needs to buy in to the battles and feel a personal commitment to the agenda that will take the business forward.

Unless you establish understanding and ownership now, while you are still at the kick-off event, the commitments made can quickly recede into memory as the event becomes just another nice initiative that did not lead to anything. While committing to one agenda before you leave does not guarantee success back at the office, it does establish a critical base for the leader to drive the journey forward into the execution phase. This step is thus a necessary, but not sufficient, condition for long-term success.

The process

As the team begin to explore the detail of what it will take to win the battles – and identify the resource trade-offs that will be necessary – there will inevitably be managers who see themselves gaining or losing power, resources, and influence. Naturally, they will start thinking about themselves and their position in the organization, and what they will tell their respective teams when they get back to the office. For the leader, this focus on "me" can be dangerous. You need to create a new mind set that gets everyone focused on the overall success of the business, and how great it will feel to be a part of that success. Your goal is to get everyone's ego tied to a common agenda.

The key elements in doing this are as follows:

1. Assign the ownership of each MWB to specified individuals, and have them build the understanding of what it will take to win their MWB. A leader needs to be assigned to each battle and then each leader needs to further examine what it will take to win that battle, and share that understanding with the whole team.

2. Commit to work together as a team to realize the MWBs. The whole group needs to discuss how they are going to work together to become a more effective management team. Clarity is needed on what the "rules of engagement" will be and what behaviors they need to adopt (and stop) to achieve their goals.

3. Commit to the agenda as individuals. Each individual needs to commit to carrying out the actions required to support the MWBs and to play his or her part in the creation of an effective team. A note of caution: as we said earlier, individual buy-in should be freely and willingly given, and not be the result of coercion. If an individual is clearly not happy with the new agenda, do not force him or her to pretend that they are – have a private discussion that may result in the manager in question taking a new role, inside or outside the business.

One week is not long enough to create a truly lasting commitment to a set of MWBs and new ways of working together, but if you manage the process well, you can establish a strong basis to build on when you get back to the office. To maximize your chances of success, we suggest that the final phase of your kick-off event follows (at least approximately) the process outlined in Figure 6.1.

In the remainder of this chapter we will discuss each of the steps in turn.

Taking ownership

Up to this point, even though the debates have been thorough (and heated at times), the MWB list is probably still a relatively abstract creation: agreed by all, owned in full by none. Now is the time to expand and deepen the group's ownership of the MWBs. To do that you first need to ensure that everyone really understands the implications of the MWB choices that have been made. Then you need ownership at two levels. At the individual level, each person needs to be committed to do his or her part in ensuring victory in the battles with which she

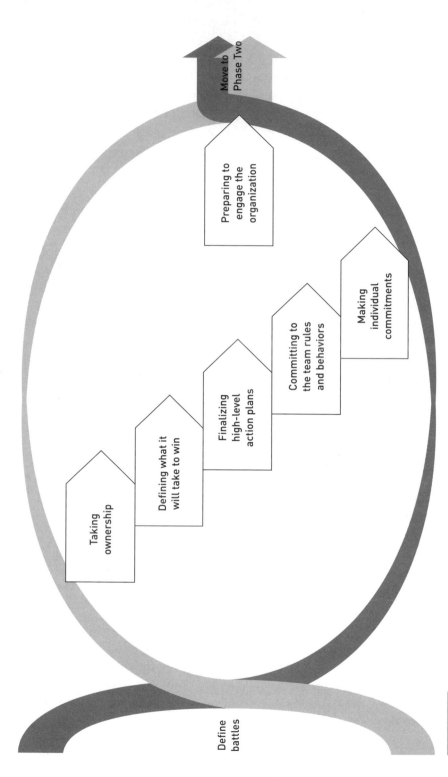

Figure 6.1 Owning and committing to one agenda: key process steps

will be most immediately involved. At the group level, you need to create a shared desire to build a genuine team that will deliver all of the battles successfully. So every member of the team needs to "own" the whole agenda – which means both buying into all of the MWBs and committing to new ways of working together.

Whether you are thinking of the team as a whole or each individual, what makes for genuine ownership is the same. Our experience suggests that you need several elements:

1. *Understanding:* the group must build a common understanding of the implications and challenges associated with each MWB, and with the collective set of MWBs.

2. *Responsibility:* individual and group responsibilities need to be clearly spelled out.

3. *Accountability:* responsibility alone is not enough; the group and each individual needs to be held accountable by the rest of the team for progress on delivering the targets. "Oh, I thought Fred was doing it," with no follow-up on whether he actually is, does not work.

4. *Authority:* without authority over resources and decisions, the owner of a battle is not likely to achieve much; he or she needs the freedom to operate quickly and effectively as needed.

5. *Buy-in:* the leader of each MWB needs to be personally committed to its overall goals and be clear that he or she has bought into the specific targets for that MWB, even though these may be aspirational.

As we have said, the starting point for building ownership is to identify the managers who will form the nucleus of the leadership team for each MWB, although one should clearly be "the" leader for the battle as our experience suggests that "single-point" leadership and accountability is important for effective implementation. An ideal MWB leader will have good knowledge of the MWB territory and a high level of credibility with the people in the organization who will later be involved in the MWB. Because MWBs are not won in a day, these MWB leaders will also have a lot of personal energy, together with the ability to create energy in others, both at the kick-off event and back at the office. The other members of the core team for that MWB will normally have skills or experience that are both relevant to the battle and complementary to those of the leader.

Most MWB leaders will take up their new responsibility with excitement, particularly if they have been fully engaged in the kick-off event and believe the MWB will play a critical role in determining the company's future. Of course, the excitement may be mixed with some trepidation because leading an MWB is a big – and very visible – challenge. However, if a potential MWB leader resists the role, it may indicate that there are still unresolved issues: for example, the new leader may be more junior than others at the kick-off event and may need assurance that he or she will have the full support of the CEO. Don't gloss over such hesitation, or force an unwilling person into a leadership role. It is important to make sure you have the right people in place. You may even have to call on someone who is not at the kick-off event to become an MWB leader. In such a case the CEO will normally play the leadership role for that particular MWB for the last two days of the event, and then "recruit" the new leader after returning to the office.

identify the managers who will form the nucleus of the leadership team for each MWB

The new MWB leaders will play a prominent role during the remainder of the kick-off event, ensuring that the MWBs are truly understood by the whole group, and leading a small sub-group, their "MWB team," in developing a first-draft, high-level action plan for their MWB, and presenting it to the group. A complete MWB action plan cannot be developed during the kick-off event because it will take time, and usually an expanded group of people to collect all of the necessary information and work through the options for going forward. So later, back at the office, the MWB leaders must expand both the action plans and the group driving the MWB.[1] The MWB leaders must also ensure that the MWBs remain at the top of the leadership team's agenda as the business moves forward. We will say more about this in Chapter 7.

[1] Not everyone who is involved in a leadership team at the event will continue to be involved with the MWB afterwards as it simply may not make sense in terms of the capabilities needed for the MWB. What is most important is to tap into each person's ideas and expertise fully at the event, as they will be instrumental in creating and maintaining positive momentum behind the MWBs across the broader organization.

Defining what it will take to win

You might well think that you had done sufficient work on defining the MWBs when you went through the selection process the previous day – moving from a long list of MWBs to the current shortlist. However, we invariably find that when the small group of people who will actually drive the MWB forward and be responsible for winning or losing the battle scrutinize their MWB, perspectives change. The MWB leaders start to feel that this is no longer just an interesting debate about priorities, this is getting real. Careers and future prospects could hang in the balance. Each MWB is now being examined by its new owners, if you will, and they want to make sure before they sign on irrevocably that this battle will be inspiring – not just to them but also to others back at the office – and winnable.

The teams leading the MWBs now need to create a first draft of a high-level action plan. The starting point is to pull out the rough action plan created earlier in the week when the MWB was first identified, and revisit it to ensure that it still makes sense. Again, we often find the teams applying a much deeper level of intensity and thought than they gave to the early draft. They are taking the first steps in creating a plan that they will be intimately involved in delivering and for which they will be held responsible – it focuses the mind.

The action plans should include four components.

- The scope of the MWB and the vision of victory.
- The external challenges that must be overcome.
- The internal challenges that must be overcome.
- Early action steps.

MWB scope and vision of victory

To get the new MWB team off to a positive start, and to avoid an early focus on the possible difficulties, we usually ask the leaders to define the scope of the MWB (i.e. what is included and what is not) and what success would look like, including the expected time frame for victory. The purpose of this exercise is to enhance and solidify the commitment of the team leaders. They need to get excited about the vision of victory that they are creating, so they can later convey that excitement to others. By way of example, the definition of success in Table 6.1 was created by one of Jan's MWB teams.

Table 6.1 Example definition of success for an MWB

Must-win battle

Within five years have 25 percent of revenues and profits coming from the ten countries, including Poland, Hungary, and the Czech Republic, that have recently joined the EU.

Using plain and simple language (i.e. no jargon), how would you describe success to a friend or your spouse?	In just three years we have grown from nothing to a top three player in eight of the ten countries that joined the EU in 2004. We are on track to be number one in five of the markets with sales of our core brand. The only places we are struggling are Slovakia and Latvia because of some distribution problems. Overall, we broke even by the end of last year. And it looks like we will be profitable this year. It's been a great success so far and everyone is really excited about the progress. Even head office.
What does success look like after one year and longer term?	By the end of year one, the company's core brand and products will be established in the 5–7 most important markets (in terms of size and growth). Consumer awareness and positive perceptions of value for money and quality will be increasing rapidly, as will sales. Smaller local competitors will be shrinking. There will be a clear path and plan to achieve profitability after three years. By the end of year five, 25 percent of Europe's revenues and profits originate in the ten target markets. The company is one of the clear leaders versus local and multinational competitors in some, but not necessarily all, markets. New regional production plant(s) and distribution centers are up and running.
What specific measures should be used to track progress?	Core measures will include absolute revenues and profits, by market and for the region overall, versus total revenues and profits for the European region. Relative growth on both dimensions in each market versus the overall region and versus key competitors will also be critical. Additional market-focused measures will be market share (by market, by product, overall), brand/product awareness, consumer perceptions of value for money and quality versus the competition, revenue and profit growth by product line/brand, margins by product/brand and by target market.

Internally focused measures will include establishment of the required organization to drive growth; set-up of production and distribution facilities to time and to budget; strength of relationships with key suppliers, customers, and outside bodies (e.g. government, NGOs); product time to market (order to shelf); time from market entry to breakeven/profitability.

If joint ventures or acquisitions are undertaken, measures will also include the success and timeliness of integrating these ventures with core operations.

What are the consequences of failure?	Potential decline in contribution of European sales and profits to overall company results, as core markets in North America are slowing.
	Declining sales and profits plus loss of market leadership in Europe overall. Failure in the new EU markets will impact on core Western European markets negatively because we fail to match consumer awareness and scale/cost advantages of key competitors that succeed in the target countries.
	A demotivated organization, under substantial pressure from headquarters where cutting costs becomes the main focus versus growth. The potential for management (us) to lose their (our) jobs!

Identify external challenges

There is not usually enough time or information to do a full-blown analysis of the external challenges that each team will encounter in the pursuit of its MWB during the offsite event. So this exercise is much more about identifying questions that need to be addressed after the offsite than providing answers. Answers, if there are any at this point, will be sketchy and partial.

To help managers generate a focused set of questions and organize their analysis we give each MWB team the simple model shown in Figure 6.2. Very often, it takes only an hour or so to generate a lot of very relevant questions, and these can later be tested with the whole group when the high-level action plans are presented. The questions then become part of the follow-up agenda back at the office.

One of Jan's MWB groups came up with the set of observations and questions in Table 6.2 when they tackled the external challenges exercise.

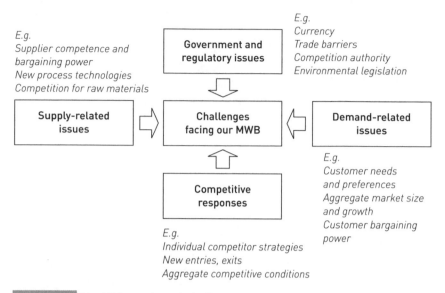

E.g.
Supplier competence and
bargaining power
New process technologies
Competition for raw materials

E.g.
Currency
Trade barriers
Competition authority
Environmental legislation

Government and
regulatory issues

Supply-related
issues

Challenges
facing our MWB

Demand-related
issues

Competitive
responses

E.g.
Customer needs
and preferences
Aggregate market size
and growth
Customer bargaining
power

E.g.
Individual competitor strategies
New entries, exits
Aggregate competitive conditions

Figure 6.2 Identifying external challenges

Table 6.2 Example: external challenges for an MWB

What are the overall external challenges we will face in addressing the MWB?	The biggest challenge – and the first one we need to tackle – will be gaining a good understanding of the marketplace (consumers, suppliers, competitors, distribution, production opportunities, regulations) so realistic market entry plans can be formulated and, if appropriate, JV or acquisition targets can be identified.
What are the key government and regulatory challenges?	We need to develop relationships with key government and NGO agencies rapidly, as some markets are still tightly regulated and in some cases we may end up competing with public or newly privatized (sometimes protected) entities. The key question is how best to do this: by ourselves (we will need to build capabilities), through local partners, through JVs, or acquisitions? We also need to get familiar with the whole range of regulations we need to observe – fast – so we can begin moving products in, probably on an export basis to start with, until we can establish local operations.
What are the major demand-related challenges?	For market entry, we will again need to gather information to be able to decide key priorities, i.e.: ● Which market(s) first, e.g. biggest, least regulated, least competitive? What are the pros and cons of different courses of action, e.g. going "head to head" in the

largest markets versus starting with a smaller market where competitive pressure will be less to allow us to build learning about the region?

- How do we roll out our presence to further markets?
- What entity we use to enter/roll out, e.g. alone, JV, acquisition?
- Who will be our target customers?
- Do we need to tailor the products to local markets?
- How do we build our brand with the consumer (marketing and PR plans)?

What are the major supply-related challenges?	Again we need more information quickly to determine how best to establish operations on the ground, i.e.: • What organization/personnel is required to support our plans? We think we should start on an export basis to test the market reaction. This means at least a sales and marketing presence in each priority country. • Where/when do we establish our own production and distribution facilities? We will need regional production capability as demand increases, to bring costs down. The team will need to do cost-benefit analysis on the possible locations and timing under a range of demand scenarios. • What channels/logistics do we need to reach target customers? • What suppliers should we use? We know there is potential for local supply but need to assess quality and reliability. • How does the technology relate to what we use in our current markets? Right now, we think the technology lags that used in Western European markets, largely for cost reasons. But we should count on the technologies converging rapidly, i.e. the need for upgrades in the new markets, once cross-border trade barriers are removed.
What are the big issues on competitor response?	We have to move fast, as multinational and regional European competitors are also planning entry and/or expanding their presence in the new EU countries. As we develop plans we should take a view on the possible strategies of our key competitors. Our starting view is to target a smaller market first to build learning about the region. However, we first need to run the numbers and get more information, so we do not get "locked out" of key markets by entering later than major competitors, who tie up key customer accounts and suppliers.

Identify internal challenges

Most new MWB teams conclude that the major internal challenges standing between them and victory have to do with acquiring new resources and developing new organizational capabilities. Simply put, the business does not yet have the resources and capabilities it will need to win that particular battle.

Resources

We usually ask each team to consider the resources they will need in the following categories, even if they cannot yet put an amount or time frame against the need for each:

- Market related, e.g. sales force coverage, distribution channels, brand reputation, product distinctiveness.
- Operations related, e.g. access to low-cost inputs, supplier relationships, plant configurations and locations, product quality, supply chain infrastructure.
- R&D related, e.g. expertise in specific technologies, new product pipeline, links to regulators.
- Financial, e.g. capital, cash flow, investor expectations, banking relationships.
- Human resources, e.g. experience and skills of key managers, union relationships, morale.
- Corporate reputation, e.g. reputation as a corporate citizen or alliance partner, relationships with the broader business community and governmental stakeholders.

When this is done, the next step is to carry out a rough "gap analysis." This means comparing the resources you already have against those that you have concluded you will need to win your MWB and identifying the key gaps. The challenge, of course, is to find ways to fill the gaps in the time available. One of Jan's teams concluded, for example, that they would very quickly have to build a distribution network in the new EU countries, either their own or through third parties. They also knew they needed to hire people with experience in these markets within three months.

Capabilities

Even more difficult than acquiring new resources is developing new organizational capabilities. As we described in Chapter 5, there is a difference between the resources a firm has and what it is capable of doing with them. Two companies may each have a development department of thirty people, for example, but if one can produce new products in half the time of the other and with twice the success rate, that is a superior capability. The thirty people are the resource but the organizational capability, which is usually a function of how they work together, is what they are capable of doing.

To get your teams thinking about the capabilities required to win each battle, suggest questions such as the following:

● What capabilities are we going to need to win our MWB?

● Which of these capabilities do we already have, for example speed in the innovation process, low cost base, or ability to work across internal barriers?

● Where are our most important capability shortfalls?

● How could we develop the new capabilities we need in the time we have available?

These questions will result in each team carrying out a capabilities gap analysis, which is a much more difficult exercise than a resource gap analysis, because capabilities are based on the behavior of people in the organization. Changing behavior – the way people work together, for example – is not straightforward, and often takes a long time. So answering the last question is extremely difficult, as the one thing you know for sure is that you will not develop new capabilities overnight.

Jan's new EU markets team had two major areas of concern about capabilities: speed, where they knew they would have to move faster than they had ever done before, and the ability to work effectively across internal boundaries. Both capabilities would be critical to the successful establishment of strong positions in the new markets. The question was how to improve them.

Early actions

Once the external and internal challenges have been identified, each team needs to put together the early steps of an action plan that will address the challenges. The danger at this point is that they could become overwhelmed by the magnitude of the task in front of them. That is why we suggested that they start their plan preparation by focusing on their vision of success for their MWB. They should open with this vision when they present their proposed high-level action plan to the larger group, as described in the following section.

Finalizing high-level action plans

Each MWB team now has a first draft of the high-level action plan that will guide "their" battle and it is time to share the potential payoffs, challenges, and early action steps of their MWB with the group as a whole. There is a lot at stake in these presentations, as this is really the last chance to evaluate each MWB and decide whether the group really wants to stick with it. Because all of the MWBs that have made it this far are very attractive, the key debates are going to be about resources, capabilities, and the probability of success.

The session begins with each MWB team presenting their vision of success for their battle, their view of the challenges to be faced, the key resources and organizational capabilities to be developed, the early action steps, and the probability of success, which may have changed slightly from when the MWB made the shortlist. Even if the probability of success has not changed, it will now be presented with more conviction and ownership. When the team who will lead the battle say publicly that they have an 80 percent chance of success, it really means something.

determining must-stops is a critical step in the MWB process

What the whole group is now able to assess in some detail, for the first time, is the collective set of resources and capabilities needed to support all the MWBs, the probabilities of success, and the set of actions that will need to be going on simultaneously in the company as these MWBs get under way. Usually, something has to give. Taken in isolation, each MWB should make sense. After all, each has been through a lot of pre-screening, and is being presented to the group by a leadership team who believe in it. But in aggregate, it may be impossible to support them all, as well as all of the initiatives that are already ongoing within the business. At this point you need to discuss the "must-stops."

Determining must-stops is a critical step in the MWB process. In spite of the pain involved, most businesses find they must stop something if they are to give the MWBs the senior management attention and resources that they need to succeed. Alternatively, they must cut back on the number or scope of MWBs. At this point the questions to focus the discussion on are as follows:

1. Do we have the time, energy, and resources to support all of our proposed MWBs, and our already ongoing initiatives? If the answer is no, what shall we cut, devote fewer resources to, or delay?

2. Are there MWBs that should be dropped or combined? Where it proves impossible to free up the required resources for an MWB, because other MWBs or activities are deemed more important, it is time to revisit the battle. If it is not a high enough priority, should it be dropped completely? Or has the specific battle been implicitly included in another, meaning they should be combined?

3. Are there ongoing initiatives that should be added to the MWB list? As you discuss the previous two questions, there will almost always be times when someone says a major existing initiative "absolutely cannot be dropped." If the group agrees, then the initiative should become an MWB – if it meets the team's criteria – and something else will have to be cut.

A reminder: do not try to please everyone

You will have to accept the fact that you are going to have some disappointed managers. Some may be victims of the must-stops. Others will have their MWBs drop off the final list. But remember, the worst outcome is to end up with too many initiatives, none of which will be adequately resourced. You, the leader, will need to force the group to come to the appropriate decisions if necessary.

The list of must-stops for Jan's group all related to ongoing activities, not to the new MWBs. They concluded that they had to do the following:

1. Halt expansion plans for the Scandinavian markets, at least in the short term, as both people and cash would need to be redirected to

the proposed new brand and the new target markets which represented a much greater long-term opportunity.

2. Stop the expansion of the Iberian manufacturing plant, depending on the outcome of the detailed planning:
   - It might make more sense to expand capacity nearer to the Eastern European markets, if not establish a new production site within these markets.
   - A new manufacturing configuration might be needed to support the proposed new brand.
   - Production lines in Belgium may need refocusing to make sufficient progress on the quality issues.

3. Reduce the marketing and sales spending planned for mature markets and redirect some of this to the proposed import-fighter brand and new target markets.

Every must-stop discussion generates resistance and conflict because, as we have said, stopping anything impacts somebody's plans or power base. This is one of those moments when you need full discussion to make sure that the sensitive issues are addressed. Executives often claim later that they weren't really involved, or that they really didn't agree even at the time. There must be no such escape here. The person who feels they are losing needs to be heard and hopefully to understand why the must-stop decision is in the broader company interest. (Chapter 3 describes some approaches that we have found useful in managing these debates.)

The end of these presentations and discussions is an important moment. This is when the complete team needs to agree and take ownership of the high-level action plans and the must-stops. Now, at a single point in time, while you are all present. It is a signal and symbol that everyone should remember. You are all here and have all been involved. This is your focus for moving forward!

Committing to the team rules and behaviors

By this point in the process, everyone knows that for the journey to be successful the leadership team will need to change the way they work together. So it is time to set aside the MWB plans, and focus on identifying the new behaviors that you need: both at a group level, and on the part of each member of the team.

What you have at this point, as illustrated in Figure 6.3, is a number of small teams, each focused on a specific MWB. These teams should be cohesive and energized because they have clear shared goals, and the accountability for delivering on an inspirational MWB.[2] This is great because it is what you have been working toward. However, the last thing you want to do is create new silos by building walls around the MWB teams. Each executive needs to see him or herself as both a leader or key member of an MWB team *and* a committed member of the team that is leading all of the MWBs to bring overall victory to the business.

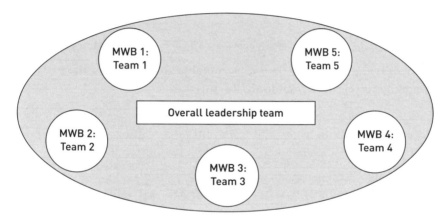

Figure 6.3 The MWB teams

The team you are trying to create will set overall priorities that provide the basis for decision making, resource allocation, and trade-offs between the MWB teams. To put it another way, the MWB teams need a hierarchy above them to resolve disputes when everyone wants the same scarce resources, to open doors as necessary for groups trying to work across organizational boundaries, and to ensure coordination between teams. An MWB leader remarked: "The measure of performance of the top team is best judged by the performance of those working below them."

[2] In "The Wisdom of Teams" (Harvard Business School Press, Boston, 1993), Jon R. Katzenbach and Douglas K. Smith state that: "A demanding performance challenge tends to create a team. The hunger for performance is far more important to team success than team-building exercises, special incentives, or team leaders with ideal profiles. . . . Conversely, potential teams without such challenges usually fail to become teams." They also suggest that if the "team basics...size, purpose, goals, skills, approach and accountability" are applied in a disciplined way these create the conditions required for performance.

Transforming a group of successful and often competitive executives into a cohesive whole that can champion and support the MWB teams is not an easy thing to do. Shifting the culture and ingrained mind set from individual performance to one of interdependence, where the collective agenda ranks ahead of individual interests, is unnatural for many people. But unless you can create a real team that buys into and begins to exhibit the required new behaviors, the MWB plans will remain unimplemented – just lists on walls.

You are not going to turn a group of competitive individuals into team players in a day, but the exercises below will get you started. We suggest you focus on:

1. Creating ground rules to govern how the team will work together.

2. Identifying "acceptable and unacceptable" behaviors for the team, and by implication each individual within it.

These exercises are also useful tools for assessing progress over time, and many leadership teams find it helpful to revisit these discussions and their outputs on a regular basis back at the office.

Exercise: leadership team roles and rules

The aim of this exercise is to begin to create in the team a sense of collective ownership of the MWB action plans. We do this by asking them what role(s) they need to play to support the plans, and of course for each individual this means we are asking how they are going to support plans for battles that are "not theirs." Thus the collective ownership begins.

Some questions that we have found to be useful discussion guides include:

● What is the role of the leadership team? What should be on the agenda of this team?

● What is *not* the role of the leadership team? What should *not* be on the agenda of the leadership team?

● What are the "golden rules" that the entire leadership team should follow to carry out their role effectively?

The focus is on the role of the leadership team after everyone is back at the office. They will need to decide, for example, how performance against the MWB action charters will be managed and monitored, how they will run their meetings, and how they will communicate with each other and the organization about MWB progress. They need to give thought to how they will build and sustain the energy that the team and organization will need to drive the battles forward.

The final discussion on golden rules usually falls naturally out of the earlier conversations on roles. As the group debates there will be certain activities or behaviors that everyone agrees are fundamental to the way the team operates and, as such, non-negotiable. At the end of the exercise the group normally agrees that there will be consequences for anyone not living up to the golden rules.

The output from Jan's team's discussions was as follows:

Leadership team – it is our role to:

- Demonstrate visible commitment of the team to the MWBs – we must be "passionate champions".
- Create a positive feeling of forward momentum; in some areas we should encourage greater risk taking.
- Ensure clear and aligned targets, goals, and milestones, communicated to all.
- Simplify and accelerate decision making, in particular on resource allocation, to reflect our priorities.
- Provide the teams with appropriate levels of authority, resources and support to do what they need to do – facilitate, not control.
- Establish – and keep to – structured progress updates for each MWB.

Leadership team – it is not our role to:

- Micro-manage each MWB – we must delegate effectively, while holding the teams accountable.
- Revisit decisions – once the debate is done and a course of action is agreed, we must deliver on it.
- Second-guess – we must not second-guess our teams' decisions.
- Create bureaucracy – we must streamline processes and speed up decisions and actions.
- Focus on short-term results – we must be guardians of the bigger picture.
- Advance our personal agendas – we must focus on the overall benefits for the company.

The golden rules

- Confront and address reality honestly.

- See change as an opportunity not a threat.

- Support each other.

- Recognize efforts and achievements and communicate these widely.

- Set a positive example – model appropriate behaviors for the rest of the organization and hold each other accountable for these.

- Respect the 75 percent rule – debate openly when we disagree, but once we have made the decision, everyone must support it 100 percent.

- Learn from, not punish, failures, and encourage experimentation to generate new ideas and opportunities.

Exercise: acceptable and unacceptable behaviors

With the new roles and rules decided, the next step is to define the behaviors that each member of the leadership team will hold themselves, and all of their colleagues, accountable for. The purpose is to spell out how the team members will treat and work with each other, how they will interact during and after meetings, and how they will represent the leadership team to their own teams as well as more broadly across the organization.

The place to start is to create clear, shared definitions of the desired behaviors, and just as clear a statement on the unacceptable behaviors. These are not just words, there will be consequences for those who later revert to the old behavior and act as if this discussion never took place. We generally ask three simple questions to get this exercise under way:

- What are acceptable behaviors for members of the leadership team?

- What are unacceptable behaviors for members of the leadership team?

- How can each member support the agreed behaviors to ensure that they are practiced by all team members?

Rather than have a long-drawn-out debate on these questions, we have found that it is better to set up three large posters, one for acceptable behaviors, one for unacceptable behaviors, and one for ideas on how to enforce or support the items on the other two posters. Give the group pens and time to write. If a behavior is already listed on the board, have people put a checkmark next to it. You will quickly begin to see those behaviors that the group wants to support, and those that it wants to eliminate.

Often the items on the lists can sound very general, predictable, or even trite. Do not worry about that. The point is that these are the behaviors that this group of executives have agreed they will hold each other accountable for, and to which they each agree to be held accountable. It is their list. There may well be overlap with what has emerged from the previous exercise, but this serves only to reinforce the agreements. Jan's group created the following list.

Acceptable behaviors:

- Support decisions made by the group 100 percent.
- Help each other meet mutually agreed goals – it is *our* problem, not just *theirs.*
- Treat each other with respect.
- Listen to different views, don't just criticize.

Unacceptable behaviors:

- Disagree with decisions made jointly, in private, or in the corridors – if you disagree, discuss it with the group in the appropriate forum.
- "Hoard" resources and people when others may need them.

How to support agreed behaviors:

- Be honest with each other when we feel someone is not demonstrating the appropriate behavior.
- Offer support and solutions rather than just criticisms, when a team member has an issue or problem.
- Revisit how well we are meeting our behavior agreements on a regular basis.
- Ask our own teams and parts of the organization for honest feedback, without "shooting the messengers."

As the group goes through these exercises, expect some resistance. You are asking people to be introspective and to examine their interactions and relationships with others. This is not an everyday activity for most business people, and you are implying, just by asking the questions, that there may be a need for change.

How should you address the resistance? First, you need to recognize that there are no "quick fixes." You can lay some foundations for behavior change, and identify and discuss issues directly during the offsite, but it will not be until the team really start working together that the collective mind set, knowledge of each other, and trust can be developed. The first challenge is to stop dysfunctional behavior. If you can do that you will have made a major step forward already, and then you can work on building collective, performance-enhancing behaviors. This is one of the reasons why we talk about MWBs as a journey and we strongly suggest you revisit the exercises in this section periodically.

Second, use every opportunity to build strong personal relationships with and between your colleagues. By this point, the group should have a much greater level of openness in their discussions than they had when they arrived at the event. They may be willing to talk about why they behave the way they do. Encourage such discussions. Also, make sure that after the event you promote a context where these personal relations can continue to grow, to build trust and mutually reinforcing excitement around collective interests. Continue to remind everyone that you have a shared dream for the future – adopting new behaviors is a major step on the road to that dream.

Making individual commitments

The behavior of your people will make or break your MWB journey. Behavior will change throughout the organization only if it changes at the top. One executive put it this way: "We will only grow as an organization and business to the extent that our people grow, and that includes our leaders." Such personal growth requires an openness to change, and the aim of this part of the event is to develop such openness by asking each individual what he or she will do to help make the MWBs and the new ways of working together a reality. Explaining the need for change in a convincing way can be difficult, but allowing people to decide for themselves how they should change their behavior, followed by input from peers, can be very powerful. Once an individual "gets it" and recognizes the personal benefit of change, the results can be energizing and exciting. We have found the spotlights exercise[3] particularly useful in leading people to recognize the need for behavior change.

[3] This exercise, referred to as "Spotlights," was introduced to us by Silvia DeVolge of the Hay Group.

the behavior of your people will make or break your MWB journey

Exercise: spotlights – making individual commitments

"Spotlights" focuses on three main questions, directed to each person at the kick-off event:

● *Actions:* what specific actions will I take to contribute to the MWB agenda?

● *Behaviors:* what behaviors will I do more of and less of to be an effective member of the leadership team?

● *Support:* what support do I need from my colleagues to help me be more effective?

Each individual starts by preparing and posting a chart which summarizes their responses to these three questions. Then the other members of their team read and prepare comments on the items on the chart. When this is done, each person takes his or her place "in the spotlight" and receives feedback from colleagues on what they have written. Although we have found that almost everyone wants to explain their responses, the exercise is most valuable when the person in the spotlight silently receives their feedback, and only at the end of their spotlight responds to what they have heard.

Normally the whole group participates in each spotlight session. But if your group is large you should consider creating sub-groups to ensure richer feedback. There is also typically a question about whether the leader should do a spotlight and, if so, when. Our answer is: most definitely yes, the leader should participate. His involvement is a critical signal to the group that he, too, is committed and wants to grow with his team. He can take his turn with everyone else, or it may be more powerful for him to make his commitments as he wraps up the session. This is what Jan did as he wanted to make an impact that would sustain the momentum as the group moved from the offsite back to the office.

Being alone in the spotlight and talking about the need to change one's behavior can be unnerving, even for the most confident of executives. This is why the discussions of support prompted by the third question can be particularly valuable. By asking about support, we make it clear that you are not alone – you are part of a team, and it is expected, and natural, that team members will support each other. It is less about admitting that you need support, rather about indicating the type of support you need. This is usually easier said than done, of course. Many people are reluctant to make such an admission of need, even at the end of the week. But usually a few brave souls will lead the way, and others will follow hesitantly. If you can guess who those brave souls will be (or can tell from what they have written on their chart), begin the spotlight exercise with them.

Preparing to engage the organization

Your kick-off event is nearly finished. On paper you have high-level action plans for each MWB, lists of leadership team roles and acceptable and unacceptable behaviors, plus individual commitments to actions and behaviors required to create a real team at the top. Even more important, you have observed the pattern of interactions among your key players toward the end of the event and this, more than anything, tells you how far you have come, and how far you still have to go.

But before you leave, you need to think about the "so what happens on Monday morning?" question. How do you ensure that the status quo does not continue? We suggest you focus on two questions:

1. How will the organization react to the MWB agenda that has been agreed?

2. What are you going to communicate to the broader organization about the MWB journey and the kick-off event?

Anticipating the organization's response

In Chapter 2 we talked about assessing the organization's starting conditions. In a nutshell the question is: how ready is the organization to embrace the MWB agenda that the team is returning with?

If you used the type of culture survey that we recommended in Chapter 2 you will have a pretty good idea of the health of your organization. Normally, a healthy organization is preferable to a returning team than one that is in disarray, but not always. If the group is coming back to a successful company and an organization that is functioning well, with an MWB agenda that calls for significant change, the organization may strongly reject the whole new initiative: "We do not need this, we are fine. These guys went crazy during the offsite." (This is why industry-leading companies are often the last to respond to fundamental shifts in their markets.) However, an organization in disarray may be able to use the new agenda to pull itself together – the MWBs become a rallying cry and a way forward.

You may also judge that some MWBs will meet much more resistance than others, and that some parts of the organization will be much more ready to buy in to the new agenda than others. So you can't generalize. What you do need to do is map the likely patterns of acceptance and resistance and plan your actions – and communications – accordingly.

Getting on message: planning first communications

Having a sense of how readily (or not) the organization will embrace the new MWB agenda will help you plan what to say when you get back. The team has been away and unreachable for a week, and the organization will have expectations about what has happened, what has been agreed, and what will come next. Remember that Monday morning will be the start of the MWB journey for those who were not at the kick-off event, and you and the team all need to be on the same page in terms of what you say, what you do, and the sense of urgency that you convey.

Before leaving the kick-off event, Jan's team created a set of communication guidelines that included the key messages that would be delivered by each of them to their part of the organization within the first few days back at work. Each person would deliver the messages in their own way, but the themes would be the same, and of course the MWBs were not up for discussion. The main messages were as follows:

1. **This is the start of a journey, not a one-off initiative**
   It is not just another initiative; it affects everything we do and means radically changing our way of working. This is not "flavor of the month" management. It will take time to implement and we are committed to making it work.

2. **It's about everything and everyone**
   We are targeting holistic outcomes for our business and our organization. It is not just about the strategic agenda, but also about how we work together at team and individual levels to achieve the results we want.

3. **These are our MWBs and their leaders**

   These are our MWBs and the leaders of each (list them) and this is why we have chosen each battle. Here are the implications of the items on this list for our part of the organization. (Present more detail on those battles most relevant to the audience being addressed.)

4. **The targets are ambitious but realistic**

   Our new targets are ambitious, but realistic. We have debated what is and is not possible in our markets and what we can aspire to, and we have listened to the cynics among us and we will listen to you too as we detail our plans further. These targets represent what we believe we can and must do to build the business and create the organization we want.

5. **We are all in this together**

   The leadership team collectively created the agenda, and we are all committed to it. It expresses what we want to achieve for the business and the organization. We will hold each other accountable for results. You should hold us accountable as well.

It had been a very long week. A week of highs, lows, and constant challenges. Many team members had resented being taken to a location without a schedule or clear objectives and being led through a "journey" whose destination was unknown. By Friday afternoon, Jan was exhausted. Not able to rely on the traditional power of his CEO position, he had often found himself struggling to lead the team through dialogs and debates, trying to reach consensus with individuals who had not agreed on anything in the past. There had been high moments when the group really seemed to understand and buy in to what Jan was trying to achieve. But there had also been times when everything seemed to fall back into the same old patterns. How much progress had really been made? Had a basis for real and lasting change been established? How far had the group really moved during this very short period? What would change when everyone got back to the office on Monday and faced the same old workplace challenges?

Although he could not answer all these questions, Jan felt that now was the time to cement in place the progress that had been made. He wanted to reinforce the ownership and commitment that he believed everyone now felt about the MWBs and the high-level action plans. He also wanted to demonstrate his commitment to follow up on what had been started. If this were to be more than just another pleasant event, the new future would have to start right here and right now.

Surrounded by his team and posters of the week's output, Jan began his final comments:

> I want to go back to the beginning of the week when I described this as a decisive moment in our history. I asked you to trust me and to trust in the process that we would be undertaking together. Now, five days later, I first want to thank each of you for the energy, commitment, and trust you have put into this week. We are exhausted but we have engaged. The week has not been easy but we have made real progress. We have entered into a new phase of working together; one that I am confident will lead us to success that we will all be proud of.

> Remember we started by talking about our hopes and fears. We all had hopes – for our business, for our team, and for ourselves. We all wanted to succeed and to create something great. We wanted to change the way we work together, getting rid of all the stuff that gets in our way. We wanted to become better leaders, better people. We wanted this event to deal with the real issues for once and not be just another complaining session where we all say the same old things. But behind these hopes were our fears and I think, for most of us, these fears were stronger than the hopes. We were afraid that this would be another case of "here we go again," following the next fad and rediscussing what we have talked about countless times before. We were afraid we could not really change, and maybe we did not even want to. We were afraid of being vulnerable in front of our colleagues.

> We then discussed how we function as a team. There are many myths that we hide behind every day. Remember the myth that we are a strong team, and the myth that our success from the past will continue because we know our customers well and are better than our competitors. Are these really true or just the stories we keep telling ourselves to keep from facing reality? How about the taboos – those things that we do not talk about openly? We can't talk about the real issues. We can't talk about our failures or weaknesses. We can't talk about how good our competitors really are. What scared me was that we as a group have been afraid to openly address the truth. As for conflicts, we considered conflict as bad for careers and something to avoid. We avoid conflict by saying yes in meetings and then objecting in the corridors afterward.

How can we ever succeed if this is our reality? Worse, if this is how we, at the top, see the situation, how does it look to the 11,500 people in the organization reporting to us? If we don't change how we, as a leadership team, work together and create an environment in which we can make progress, there is no hope for the people we are leading. This was a real wake-up call for many of us. I hope we all left those discussions with a commitment to change – I certainly did. It is our responsibility as leaders to do so. We are the only people who can do it.

We then moved on to look at our business. We all arrived here with strategies for our parts of the business. But nine strategies means no strategy. Looking at our business from our competitors' and customers' viewpoint was very, very useful. We concluded that our competitors have smart executives just like us, probably in similar rooms, thinking about how they will beat us. And our customers are fighting their own battles, in which we may or may not be helping them. Remember the passion we had when we took their perspectives. Why was it easier to feel that passion when we stepped outside our own business? We know our business in our guts and in our hearts. We must get that same energy and passion into our own organization.

Next, we looked inside and thought deeply about what we want to leave behind. Remember our words: Fast-moving! Innovative! Exciting! Can-do attitude! We are not those things today. But we must be. We must leave behind a stronger and more exciting business than we inherited. This is the organization we need in order to win the battles we face.

We then got down to the hard work of defining our MWBs and what we need to do to win them. The MWBs and the action plans are the tangible output that we will take back to our people. These are not just my plans, they are owned by all of us; we debated and agreed on them together. But now the time for debate is over. It is time for implementation – taking action, winning in markets.

Finally, and most importantly, we talked about the way we work together. In the end, the way we behave will determine our success. Look at our agreements on these charts:

1. What has been agreed on in meetings must not be subverted later in private.
2. No hidden personal agendas, the company comes first.
3. Trust and support colleagues.
4. Tell the truth.

Why have these very simple standards been so hard to live up to? The only thing that will make these behaviors a reality is if we all hold each other accountable for them. If any of us do not live up to them, including me, it is the right – and obligation – of each of us to challenge that person. Nothing will change if we allow ourselves to fall back into our old ways.

We have now come to the end of our event. I am not sure about the rest of you, but I am exhausted yet very excited about the future. If we can harness the energy and commitment that we created this week, there will be no stopping us. We all want to be part of a winning team. The way forward is now clear. All we have to do is do it.

I wish you all a safe trip home and look forward to seeing you on Monday!

Section

Making it happen

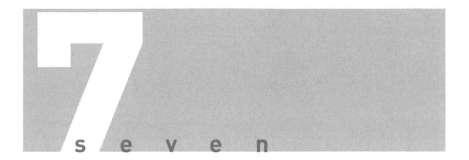

Engaging the organization

Maria (two weeks after returning to the office):

I left the kick-off event with a lot of hope. Like everyone else, I really believed in our MWBs. For the first time we all were aligned and committed to the same agenda. And we had developed trust in Jan and in each other, so some barriers had definitely been broken. We were convinced we could make a difference, and we all knew what we had to do. I was looking forward to delivering my progress report at our first meeting.

But when I got to the office, there were more than 200 emails waiting for me, and 30 telephone calls to return. My sales teams were virtually lined up outside my door, pressing me to make decisions that had been piling up the previous week. I felt swamped. I knew the MWBs were important and I was convinced I would get to them, just not today.

By the time the first MWB meeting rolled around, I was embarrassed by how little I had done. But it soon became obvious that I was not the only one who had not moved far on the new agenda, in spite of the promises we had made to each other. We were all too busy handling the nitty-gritty details of keeping the company running. In the meeting we reverted to our old behaviors, blaming everyone and everything except ourselves for our lack of progress. The spirit and energy of just a couple of weeks ago seemed a long way away. We were all thinking: had all this effort been for nothing? Did we really have just another off-site that would soon be forgotten?

Leadership teams coming back from MWB kick-off events are usually tired, but at the same time energized and optimistic about the MWB agenda and the commitments that everyone has made to work together differently. There is a new sense of energy, clarity, and urgency. But the first days back at the office are often a rude awakening. Moving from an energizing one-week event to beginning a company-wide transformational journey is a big challenge.

Enthusiasm and hope are often met with skepticism from colleagues who were not at the event and remained mired in the day-to-day realities of running the business. "So you had a good time. Welcome back to work." Or, "You sound just like you did when you came back from that leadership team-building session last year." On top of this you will find the "operational swamp" is very real. Daily tasks and deadlines start to suck up your time and energy. Maria's backlog of emails and phone messages is not at all unusual, nor are subordinates with urgent decisions that must be made and agendas of their own that they want to move forward. The MWB promises are often put to one side "for later, when I have more time."

So how do you navigate the swamp and start to engage the organization to make the MWB agenda happen? Figure 7.1 gives an overview of Phase Two of the journey.

There are three important stages required to convert a good kick-off event into the beginning of a transformational journey:

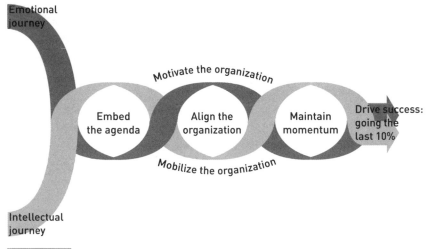

Figure 7.1 The MWB journey – Phase Two: building blocks for engaging the organization

1. **Embedding the agenda in the organization:** putting in place all of the "pieces" necessary to transform the MWBs from a list of priorities agreed at an offsite meeting into the central strategic agenda that will drive the leadership team and the whole organization forward.

2. **Aligning the organization**: involving all parts of the company in the journey, by cascading the MWB agendas throughout the organization. Change requires more than ownership and involvement at the top, it requires commitment and aligned actions across the entire organization.

3. **Maintaining momentum**: continuously reinforcing the new agenda across the organization and reaccelerating MWBs that are not progressing. The MWB journey is not a six-month affair. As time passes you have to continue to make it clear through your words and deeds that the MWBs are not just a fad. Strong commitment at the top must be ongoing.

We will discuss each stage in turn before we return to the final challenge highlighted in Figure 7.1: what it means to go the last 10 percent that will determine ultimate success.

Embedding the agenda

The first three months back at the office are critical. People are busy, definitely not waiting for you to suggest new and different things for them to do, and there is a very real possibility that the MWB agenda will never take hold and become part of the organization's day-to-day reality. The leadership team need to find ways to ensure that the MWB agenda moves to the heart of the business, and if this is not happening by, say, the end of the third month, it probably won't.

The first step is to embed the new agenda into the ongoing activities of the leadership team and what you judge to be the key areas within your organization. This needs to be done quickly, while your team members still remember the promises they made at the kick-off event, because in spite of their claims to the contrary, many will take comfort in diving back into the familiar details and everyday issues that they are so good at, and putting the MWBs to one side.

To embed the agenda you need to focus on four tasks. The first is **communicating the MWB agenda** to the rest of the organization. You will be communicating both the MWBs and the leadership team's commitment to them. The second involves **building the action plans** for each MWB; taking the high-level plans developed during the kick-off event and fleshing them out to create the detailed plans required to drive action. The detailed plans will also later become the basis for evaluating progress toward winning each battle. The next job is to **institutionalize the agenda**, which means integrating the MWB priorities into the everyday operational activities of the company. The final task is to **free up time and resources** for the journey ahead. If you simply add the new agenda on top of existing ones, you will create frustration and conflicting priorities – and the sort of initiative overload Jan found when he took over as CEO. If the MWBs are the critical priorities, then something else must give way, as time, resources, and energy are finite.

Communicating the MWB agenda

No institutional transformation takes place, I believe, without a multi-year commitment by the CEO to put himself or herself constantly in front of employees and speak in plain, simple, compelling language that drives conviction and action throughout the organization.

Lou Gerstner[1]

At the kick-off event the leadership team developed insights, made choices, and built commitments that everyone hoped would transform the way the organization would work in the future. If this vision is to become reality, the first step is to communicate it throughout the whole organization. There are two objectives in this communication: first, to share the new agenda and its implications honestly and in such a way as to motivate people to step up to the challenges ahead; second, to establish an open environment for discussion that will lead to an ongoing two-way dialog, as well as progress and problems being shared up, down, and across the organization as the journey progresses.

As you develop a communications strategy, remember that you have two target audiences. The obvious one is the broader organization, meaning everyone who was not at the kick-off event. Here, the objectives are to share the MWB agenda and what it means for the company and for people personally. The perhaps less obvious audience is the group at the kick-off event. You need to keep them focused on the

---

[1] Gerstner, Louis V., Jr. (2002) *Who Says Elephants Can't Dance: Inside IBM's Historic Turnaround*, HarperCollins, London.

new agenda because, like you, they will be the visible spokespeople and owners of the MWB journey. It has to be obvious to everyone that the leadership team has bought in. The whole organization will be watching to see whether decisions are made in line with the new agenda, if resource allocations are actually changed, and whether new behavior is really taking place. Words are important, but communication is a lot more than words. "Walk the talk" is definitely the order of the day.

Expanding communication across the organization

As we have said, communication must start as soon as the team gets back to the office, which is why we recommended in Chapter 6 that you agree on the key messages to be communicated before you leave the kick-off event. So you should be ready to begin your communications on day one back at the office, leaving no time for skepticism to grow or rumors to begin.

The team must communicate their passion and commitment to the new agenda. This means that you must go beyond email and PowerPoint presentations. Face-to-face, in-depth communication takes time, but it is vital if you really want to bring about major change. One leader whom we think did it right asked the group that had been at the kick-off event (eight people) to sit down with him and the top seventy executives in the company. The group that had been at the event explained what they had done, the experiences they had been through, the agreements they had come to (the MWBs, the leadership team roles and behaviors, the individual commitments) and how they had changed personally during the week offsite. The group then participated in a marathon question-and-answer session. Over four hours, no punches were pulled; the conversation covered both emotional and intellectual issues and each MWB was explained in as much detail as had been worked out. So everyone knew who would be leading each MWB, how much homework still had to be done, and in what areas. In total, the message coming from the team was a mix of solidarity, focus, accountability and excitement about the way forward. It was clear to all that the commitment was real; this was not a passing fad.

At the end of the session, the team and the seventy managers went to brief their individual teams. As their common script, everyone had the few slides containing the core messages that had been created during the kick-off event. Over these bare bones, each would now overlay some of the passion and commitment behind each message, as well as an indication of what needed to happen next.

Be clear though, no matter how great the team's passion and commitment to the new agenda, there will be resistance. Jan knew, for example, that the Scandinavian country teams were going to protest long and loud as their expansion plans were put on hold, and the Spanish country head might quit if the proposed plant there did not go ahead. He believed, however, that clarity and honesty were essential from the very beginning of the MWB roll-out, and made sure that he delivered the messages to the Spanish and Scandinavian teams in person soon after getting back to the office. He led each team step by step through the logic that the team had followed at the kick-off event – looking at challenges from outside-in as well as inside-out, the same process the teams would go through when the journey was cascaded through the organization a couple of months later. He also made it clear that the decisions were not reversible, and that each group had an important role to play in helping the organization to win the chosen MWBs. Both teams clearly showed their disappointment, but Jan felt that his straightforward presentation at least allowed them to understand why the decisions had been made, even if they did not like the result.

Creating an ongoing dialog

You should be able to establish the legitimacy and importance of the MWB agenda with your first wave of communication. Then you need to support it over time. In our experience, the more often you report progress the better – MWB updates should become an integral part of daily organizational life. As results come in, you should respond with visible action. Celebrate success and share learnings from failures – your quick response and honesty will enhance the credibility of the journey and encourage commitment to it.

MWB updates should become an integral part of daily organizational life

Our advice is to use more than one channel of communication to report MWB progress, so you will reach as many of your people as possible. A good example is the three-pronged communication strategy developed by Carlsberg, the Danish brewer.

Communicating about the MWB journey at Carlsberg

At the outset of the MWB journey, Carlsberg created a bi-monthly newsletter for its leaders focusing on MWB activities. At the time of writing, the newsletter (averaging 6–8 pages per issue) is just finishing its second year of publication. Each issue kicks off with a letter from CEO Nils Andersen, and presents concrete measures of progress against targets, as well as current challenges or barriers to progress. The newsletter strikes a good balance between results to date, current activities and future challenges.

Carlsberg's second communications thrust centers around the annual leadership meeting, which brings together the top 120 managers in the company. These sessions provide a forum for sharing progress on the MWB agendas and identifying and focusing the organization on the challenges ahead. The sessions are interactive, allowing everyone to be involved in the discussion of key issues. This is also a time to celebrate the MWB successes of the past twelve months. The intent is to recharge everyone's batteries, while at the same time bringing the top 120 as fully as possible into the process of driving the MWBs forward.

The third component of Carlsberg's communication strategy is to use the senior leaders as the visible "face" of the agenda. For example, executives visiting different parts of the company's worldwide operations talk about the changes under way, and what they mean for that part of the organization. These groups are smaller and the conversations more informal than those at the annual top 120 meeting, and the messages can be more specific, focused on the expected role of the individual units and the local executives. This direct personal touch builds motivation and demonstrates to the team on the ground that the senior leaders really are focused on the new agenda.

Carlsberg's three-part communication strategy works, and definitely helps maintain the momentum in a long journey. The company's management clearly understands that MWB communications cannot be "one-time events," nor can they be focused on only one part of the organization. It takes time to achieve the MWB goals, and individuals cannot achieve these working alone or even in teams within a single silo. What you need is an organization that communicates across organizational levels and boundaries, using informal as well as formal channels. It is often argued that the most effective communication means in any company is the rumor mill – so you need to get it working for you, not against you! As a final element of your communications strategy, try to get your informal opinion leaders – the ones everyone listens to – to commit early and clearly to the new agenda.

The bottom line is that effective communications are not just a "nice to have" part of your MWB journey, they are vital to your success.

Building action plans

During the kick-off event small teams created high-level action plans for each of the chosen MWBs. These plans were used to make preliminary estimates of the challenges ahead and build a common understanding as to what each battle would entail and its probability of success. However, to move to concrete action, you now require more specific road maps with clear action steps, resource needs, and measurable targets mapped out over time. Basically, you need to work out the details of what, when, where, and how for each battle – as quickly as you can. Each MWB team should be asked to present detailed action plans within 1–2 months of returning to the office.

Mapping the details of an MWB means being clear about the steps to be taken, but also about the people who need to be involved. Our experience suggests focused (single-point) leadership is very important, and the MWB leader should be directly accountable to the leadership team, who in turn need to ensure that he or she has the resources required to take action. Most MWB leaders will have been determined at the kick-off event, and each will have worked on a high-level action plan with colleagues there. But not all of those colleagues will continue to be a part of that MWB team. Other people with different skills and interests will be required to complete the planning and to take the required actions. So each MWB plan should indicate who these people are and how their time will be freed up to join the team. As a general rule, MWB teams should be small, to ensure close collaboration, energy, and agility, but balanced enough to include all of the perspectives that will impact the battle (e.g. functions, geographies, products, and so on). We often find that MWB teams expand over time, as more parts of the organization become engaged in the battle.

Most companies have established approaches for building detailed action plans so we will not go into depth on such processes here. We do suggest, though, that you revisit some of the questions discussed at the kick-off event and push these down to the next level of specificity. For example, what resources and organizational capabilities will be required to win each battle? Where are the gaps versus what we have today, and which gaps are key? How do we fill them? Are the external challenges what we expected they would be, now that we have done more analysis? Are the stakeholder positions really as we thought, after further discussions with them? And so on.

Be careful that this plan preparation does not turn into an internally focused, number-crunching, intellectual exercise. Challenge each team to take customer and competitor perspectives. Ask them to visit markets and talk to customers and consumers. They should also visit colleagues across the company to tap into the knowledge and insight that exists inside the organization. At the same time they can use these visits to create involvement, buy in, and support of the different parts of the organization that will be involved in winning the battle.

Don't forget that the detailed action plans must be prioritized and focused and not just be a laundry list of actions. The same principles that applied in defining the MWBs also apply here:

1. Be clear and focused about the critical actions that must be taken to succeed in the MWB. Lack of prioritization is a common pitfall at this point in the process.

2. Make sure that the people involved in each MWB take a holistic view of the actions required to win that battle. The individual actions (or supporting battles) are nearly always interconnected, so everyone needs to be aware of those interconnections and take care that working to win their piece is not at the expense of the others.

3. Ensure that the individuals involved in the battle understand that they will be required to work in teams across internal boundaries, so they will need to adopt a new, more inclusive mind set and behave in ways they may never have done before.

Institutionalizing the agenda

You have now communicated the outcome and commitments from the kick-off event to the broader organization. The MWB teams are developing detailed action plans. What else must you do to transform the MWBs into a living mandate for the decisions, actions, and behaviors of the leadership team, and the whole organization? What else is required to move from a nice event to a journey?

The answer is that without clear accountability (and consequences) for MWB-related success and failure, not much is likely to happen. The MWB agenda needs to be built into the organization's formal processes – the budgeting, planning, and reward systems – as quickly as possible. Progress on the MWBs should be reviewed and discussed at each leadership team meeting.

MWBs on the leadership team agenda

In an early communication session, Jan was asked how often the leadership team would monitor progress against the new targets. His immediate response – which was the right one – was that it would be at the top of the agenda at every leadership team meeting. Each MWB leader, whether a member of the leadership team or not, would be asked to report his or her results on a regular basis to this group. Like many other companies, Jan's team decided to adopt a scorecard for tracking the progress of each MWB. The performance indicators for each battle (which would be defined in the detailed action plans) would be reported at every meeting in terms of green, yellow, and red lights on a single page. Green would indicate that results were progressing according to plan. The team would not discuss these items in any detail, except to identify challenges ahead. Yellow would show that results were within 10 percent of targets, with plans in place to achieve the targets. The items might not need discussion immediately, but awareness would have been raised of potential issues ahead. Red would indicate that results were below target, and this was where in-depth discussions would take place. Everyone felt that this approach would let the team focus their time and energy on those issues that demanded their attention.

This formalization of the "hard" side of the MWB agenda is an important step. But there is a second, much softer agenda that also needs to be monitored. This relates to the promises that your group made to each other at the kick-off event about how they were going to begin to work together as a real team. So you should revisit the acceptable and unacceptable behaviors agreed at the event and ask each other and yourself honestly: how am I doing against these standards of behavior that we set ourselves? How are we doing together? Have things really changed? Are we making progress toward the organizational legacy that we said we wanted to pass on?

The leader has an important role to play in these discussions, both in making sure that they happen and in creating the right environment for honest debate and reflection. Many have found that this includes leaving room for regular one-on-one "fireside chats" with members of the team. Mutual trust can be built during these sessions, making issues easier to recognize and diffuse early. The CEO of one major corporation decided to hold an hour-long "chat" every month with each of his executive team, with the team member setting the agenda. This meant that the executive could discuss any business issues, whether MWB related or not, on which she or he wanted the CEO's advice or input, but on the clear understanding that the person was running their own show and would make the final decision. Often, the hour was spent on more personal discussions, with the CEO and the executive simply getting to know each other better. Over time, these "chats" helped to shift the culture at the top dramatically, from one of competing silos to one of cooperation and mutual trust. In this changed environment, the cross-boundary MWB teams were able to operate much more effectively, and both morale and performance improved significantly.

Building the MWBs into core business processes and systems

In addition to putting the MWBs front and center in every leadership meeting, they must be incorporated into the budgeting, planning, and reward systems of the company. One of the key differentiators between companies that have sustained momentum on their journey versus those that have not is the extent to which they have done this. In most companies budgeting and planning processes are at the heart of the resource allocation process, so if the MWBs are to get the resources they need, they must be reflected in these systems – across the whole organization, not just at the top.

At least as important as budgeting and planning processes are your reward and recognition systems, which have a profound impact on behavior. So you need to think carefully about how teams and individuals will be rewarded for progress on the MWBs, not just financially but in terms of visibility, recognition, and opportunity. One important indicator of your leadership team's commitment to the MWB agenda, for example, is the percentage of variable compensation that will be based on team, rather than individual, performance. If you say that the MWB agenda is your priority, and that you will win your MWBs only if your people behave as a team, but then reward executives for individual performance, the credibility of the MWB agenda will be completely undermined. If you want to change people's behavior, you will probably have to change the way you pay them. If you want teams, pay for team-based results.

Freeing up time and resources

As we have said, launching a new agenda into an already busy organization is very difficult. Unless you have an organization that is operating well below its capacity, some ongoing activity is going to have to stop. It may be that you do not have enough resources – perhaps money, or the time of critical people – to support everything. Or it may be that initiatives are under way that do not fit with the MWBs – maybe some will even undermine the MWBs by sending mixed messages to your customers. Whatever the reason, there will be things that you have to stop.

Your leadership team discussed this issue at the kick-off event and agreed what the "must-stops" would be, so now is the time to actually do it. This will not be easy, and you will hear a lot of special pleading as to why "my project should be saved." Debates that you thought were finished will be reopened. But you have to act; you have to be tough. It is more fun to start things, to plan the new MWBs; it is no fun to stop things. This is exactly why firms end up with too many initiatives. So do it, and do it early. Delay will feed the hopes and build the resolve of those who do not want things stopped. You need to free up resources to support the MWB teams, and you also need to send a clear message to the organization that you are serious about the new agenda.

When you cut from the top, and assert the primacy of the MWB agenda, you are also sending the message that it is "OK to say no" to executives who are unfocused, overworked, and being pulled in all directions. They too can cut what they need to in order to focus on the MWB agenda. One executive explained:

> Until we had our own MWB-driven agenda, we were victims of everyone else's agendas. We were continually responding to others' initiatives and requests. We didn't have the ability to just say no! With our own agenda, we can now discuss and decide which activity is more important and adds more value to the company. Would it be better to spend time and energy filling in an additional form or winning in the markets? We became much stronger at pushing back. This did not mean we said no to everything, but the choice became explicit and decisions were made based on taking the

MWB forward. Our approach led to some rather strong discussions with some of my colleagues who had been sending these requests. But these were discussions that had to happen.

Aligning the organization

Let's assume that you have made a good start. Your communication process is under way, your MWB leadership teams have developed detailed action plans, and the MWBs are definitely on the leadership team's agenda and being put into the company's systems and processes. The question now is: what about the rest of the organization? How do you make sure that everyone else's priorities and activities are aligned with what has been agreed at the top? In particular, how do you ensure that the mid-level leaders across the company are buying into the new agenda? They too need to engage in the emotional and intellectual journeys and understand their role in both winning the MWBs and creating the new organizational climate. Now is the time to cascade the MWB journey down into the organization, to build ownership and alignment across the entire company.

The cascade process

Cascading the MWB agenda into the organization can be tricky. At the heart of the issue is the fact that the organization has not been built around the MWBs – and it cannot be, for the MWBs will change as time passes. The organization consists of operating units that may be based on geography, business lines, functions, and so on. There are no formal organizational units headed "MWB A," or "MWB B." The MWB leadership teams are operating outside the formal structure, and the leaders of each MWB are usually leading their battle in addition to holding down a senior position in the company.

So the challenge is to get what might be called the "silo-based" organization (including the corporate center) to buy into and actively support the MWB agenda. That agenda has two parts: the specific MWBs that must be won, and the broader organizational vision that was elaborated by the leadership team at the kick-off event. That vision will obviously impact the way the organization works together in the future, and each unit needs to decide how the vision will influence its activities and role in the organization. In effect, each unit needs to develop a sub-vision that supports the overall vision.

Each organizational unit also needs to identify and create supporting battles to advance the top-level MWBs. These supporting battles may vary substantially across business units, first because not all of the MWBs will have equal importance for or require equal involvement from all organizational units. In fact, some units may have virtually no role in certain battles, whereas others will be completely immersed in a given battle. Secondly, the market realities of each organizational unit will differ, impacting how they will define their priorities and supporting battles.

each unit needs to develop a sub-vision that supports the overall vision

A word of warning: while you of course want everyone to take emotional and intellectual ownership of their supporting battles, you do not want to create silo-based battles and teams that do not align with the overall thrust. There is a delicate balance between giving the silo-based leaders the necessary autonomy to decide how they can best support the overall company battles, and making sure they stay aligned. In practical terms, this is best achieved through face-to-face discussions; so members of the leadership team(s) of each company-level MWB should be present at silo-based MWB cascade events, both to explain the detail of the battle and to help align supporting battles with the larger one.

The cascading process starts at the top and normally works across the organizational units and down through the organizational layers. In each unit, the approach is simultaneously to build the team and the action agendas, just as the leadership team did. The key stages used in the kick-off event are equally important at every level: opening windows, defining and agreeing on battles, and committing to one shared agenda. However, the discussions should be tailored to the situation facing each unit and its respective team. Plus, the starting point is fixed – you do not go back and revise the vision and MWB agenda of the higher layers; these are taken as given. But you do need to explain them.

So at the start of each cascade, ensure that a member of the leadership team is present to explain the overall MWB agenda, talking about not just the decisions taken to create it but also how they were reached and how they are being moved forward. This discussion should also provide the opportunity for the MWB team leaders to share the required detail about each battle, as noted above, as well as the new ways of working and behaviors needed to underpin it. The presence of the leaders from the "next level up" is critical, as it makes the debates more productive and questions about the overall agenda can be answered on the spot, eliminating the potential for misunderstandings that could require later reworking of some supporting battles. In addition, relationships can be built as everyone works together on aligning the agendas, so feel part of the same team, reinforcing the collective view of the business. The newly appointed leaders of supporting battles will become part of the team for the relevant company-level MWB.

The actual number of cascade events you run will depend on the size and complexity of your organization. We know of a regional company in a single industry, for example, whose cascade involved three events over a three-month period: one for the company's leadership team (fifteen people), one for the leadership team of the home market (forty), and one for the leaders of the "international" operations (twenty-five). At a medium-sized global player, five sessions took place over six months. The first engaged the executive leadership team (twelve people), followed by three events for regional leadership teams (averaging thirty-five people per session), and a final session for the corporate headquarters staff (twenty-five). In a very large complex organization, the cascading process comprised eighteen sessions, involving over 500 executives over fourteen months.

An example

So how does it work? Let's return to Jan's MWB journey for a closer look. After three months back at the office, his group was making progress. The initial communication efforts appeared to have been successful, and three MWB leadership teams had been created, each of which had prepared detailed action plans. Now they needed to cascade the journey to the rest of the organization. The question was, where to start.

The European division that Jan headed was split into three geographic business units, supported by a small corporate center. The UK and Ireland unit represented the core of the company, both organizationally and financially, because like many US companies this had been the first "outpost" in Europe. Here, the company had a strong leadership position. However, competition was increasingly cut-throat. The muscle of the big retail chains, including burgeoning own-label activities, was putting pressure on margins, and the region was suffering from a rising flow of Asian imports. The Western Europe unit, on the other hand, had grown substantially over the last decade and had now overtaken the UK in terms of revenue, though not yet in profits. This region, too, faced markets that were mature and competitive, as well as being fragmented. Many strong players competed head to head, and the region was undergoing significant consolidation. Eastern Europe was the newest organizational unit, and contained the markets where the growth potential was highest. For Europe as a whole to meet the challenging objectives that headquarters had set, Eastern Europe's potential would have to be realized – and the objective of one of the MWBs was to ensure that happened.

The MWBs that had been agreed at the kick-off event would impact each of the three regional units differently. Fixing the quality (and associated cost) issues at the Belgian plant was of most concern to Western Europe, but the UK was also impacted as it was supplied by the Belgians. The anticipated growth in demand from Eastern Europe would also have to be partly supplied from this plant until new facilities were established. So while Eastern Europe's primary interest was the MWB that focused directly on its local growth, that was not the only MWB in which its leadership team had a stake. Creating a new brand to fight Asian imports was of concern to all units, because even though the UK was currently taking the hardest hit, it was simply a matter of time before everyone felt the same pressure.

Jan's team decided to begin the cascade process with the UK and Ireland unit. In terms of depth of leadership and experience it was arguably the strongest region, and while there would certainly be resistance to change there, Jan felt that if this could be overcome, the unit would be a strong ally in pushing the MWB agenda forward in the other two regions.

Jan and the three MWB team leaders all decided to attend the four-day cascade event. On the first evening, Jan described the process and the debates that had taken place at the leadership team's kick-off event, and the MWB agenda that had resulted. He made it clear that the purpose of the cascade event was not to "sell" this higher-level agenda to each part of the organization, although they did need to be aware of it. "I want you," he said, "to understand where the next level up in the organization is going in terms of its priorities and vision, to reflect on the opportunities and challenges available in your markets, and then to design (and own) an agenda that builds on local opportunities and contributes to the company's overall objectives."

Not surprisingly, like the leadership team before them, the local executives all had different perspectives on the challenges facing their business, and many conflicting points of view. They too needed to open windows and break down silos so they could establish a common perspective on the challenges and opportunities ahead, build a shared vision, and define a set of MWBs that would reflect the collective priorities of the region. By the middle of the second day, some key insights had emerged from the opening windows exercises which were captured in a new regional vision, which emphasized being best-in-class in local markets but also playing a strong supportive role across the whole of Europe. The major breakthrough came when the team, which had been focusing exclusively on the UK and Ireland growth agenda, came to the conclusion that it would make more sense for the region to become the cash "engine" for the whole division. Their cash could play an especially important role in supporting the expansion in Eastern Europe. One executive summarized:

> We have to optimize what we are doing in our local markets, but it is clear that our growth opportunities do not offer the same financial returns as those in Eastern Europe. We have opportunities to cut fat in our organization and to focus intensely on cash generation. We do not all like this option, but if we can do it, we can make a real contribution to Europe as a whole. So in a sense we have created a supporting battle – generate cash for growth – that will support the Eastern European MWB.

The group then went on to define a broader list of supporting MWBs, clearly linked to the overall MWB agenda:

1. Optimize the brand and product portfolios: reinforce the premium brands and products, and make space in the brand portfolio for the new import-fighter brand.

2. Deliver best-in-class customer value propositions: understand customer needs more deeply and leverage our local R&D and marketing capabilities to provide the input for developing the import-fighter brand, as well as knowledge which could be shared across all regions to promote growth, particularly in the new Eastern European markets.

3. Revitalize the sales process: build stronger and deeper relationships with the major retailers, again to provide the traction for the new brand, and also to mitigate margin pressure to improve cash flow.

4. Generate cash for growth: reduce the cost base to improve cash generation to drive growth across the division.

The UK and Ireland leadership team then assigned leaders for each supporting battle, developed high-level action plans, built individual and team commitment to the chosen battles, and agreed on new ways of working together. The leaders of the supporting battles would report to the UK and Ireland leadership team meetings on a regular basis, and would also be part of the overall MWB teams for the particular division MWBs that they supported.

The cascade process was quickly repeated in the other two regional units. The final result was an aligned and integrated MWB agenda, illustrated in simplified form in Figure 7.2. This overall MWB agenda of battles and supporting battles was understood and owned by the leadership teams in each region, who were now ready to take the cascade forward to the departments within their units.

Jan and the leadership team now felt that the European division was on the move. But there was one area outstanding. Although the leaders of the corporate center functions had been actively involved in many of the discussions – two were members of the leadership team and others had been involved in the cascades – the center had not yet been formally involved in the MWB process. There had already been discontented mutterings from some of the finance team who had been asked to do preparatory work for the events but felt "left out," and the central R&D function under the brilliant but mercurial Boris was critical to any new brand proposition. Another cascade was required because the center would play a key role in the success of the journey.

The role of the corporate center

Some companies focus their cascades only on their business units, and do not directly address the role of the corporate center in the MWB process. This is dangerous. The corporate center can be an important enabler of progress, supporting and linking the activities going on across the operating units, but it can also be a major barrier to progress, slowing down the entire journey.

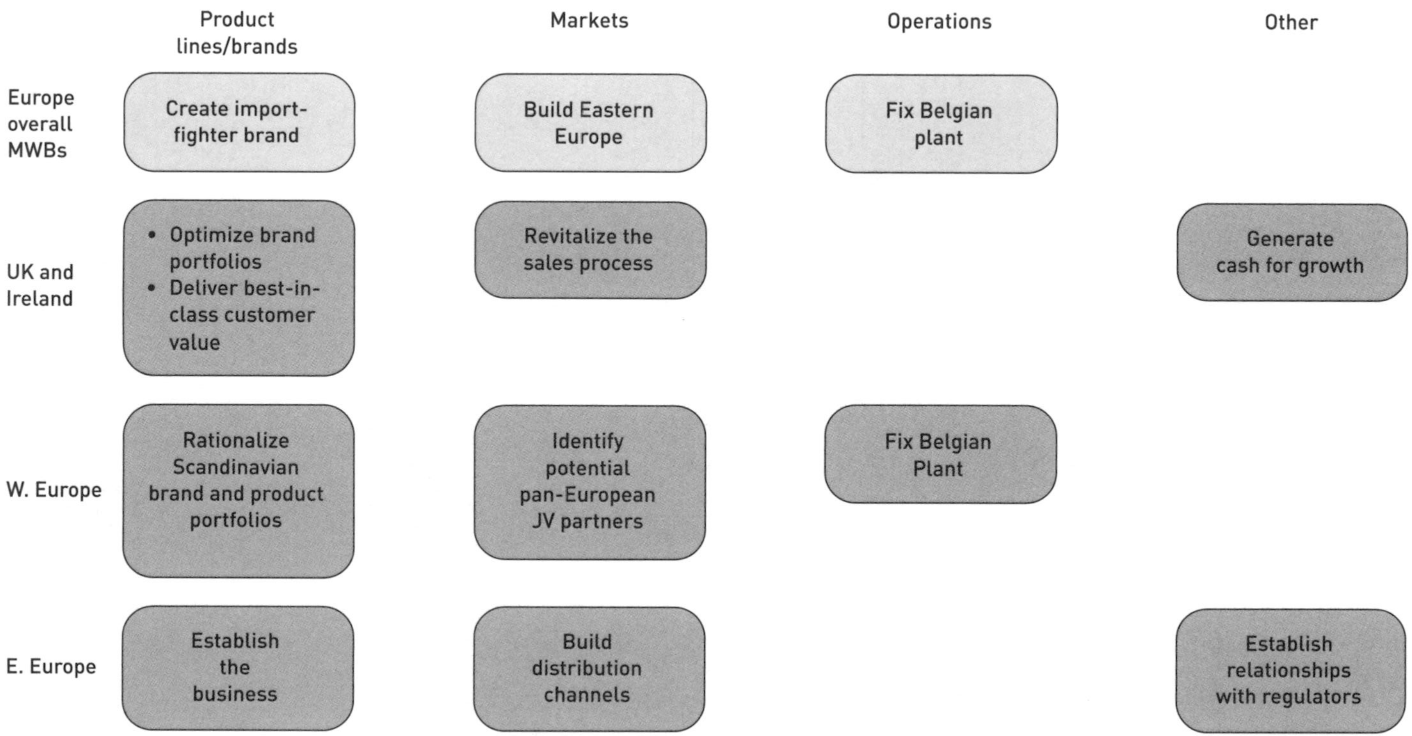

Figure 7.2 The cascaded MWB agenda

As you cascade the MWB journey, we strongly recommend two things. First, involve people from the center in the operating unit cascades. If you know that corporate R&D could be an important voice in a debate at a given cascade event, make sure you have key R&D people at the event. The same is true for any other corporate function, be it legal, finance, supply chain management, or whatever.

Second, hold a separate corporate center cascade, after the operating units have completed their cascades. The objective is not to generate more MWBs, but for the people from the center to consider the results of the operating unit cascades and work out how they can best help these units win their MWBs and supporting battles.

In addition, corporate center personnel might use these sessions to address and figure out how to overcome a high degree of cynicism among the operating units about their role and value added to the business. Jan had already heard some "classic" comments from the regional teams:

- Some of the most dangerous words you can hear are 'I am from the corporate headquarters. I am here to help.'

- What happens when you take a bunch of smart people, let them define their own jobs, and then don't hold them accountable for any results?

As Jan, the MWB team leaders, and the corporate center team worked through the cascade process, they used the overall MWB agenda set out in Figure 7.2 in conjunction with the role descriptions in Table 7.1 to clearly define the role and the objectives of the central departments.

Everyone agreed that success for the corporate center would be determined by the success of the whole division in achieving its MWBs. The center's role was to support the two "core customers" who would be driving the battles: the company management and the regional business units. For the leadership team, the center would provide effective corporate governance, drive knowledge sharing and alignment across the business units, and work to develop a high-performance culture across the organization.

The needs of the business units were quite different. They expected the center to offer expertise that could support them by providing help in areas such as R&D and negotiations with regulators in Eastern Europe. The regional units also wanted the center to establish better information flows, so that customer insight, for example, would be shared more

Table 7.1 Corporate center role descriptions[2]

Governance role	Corporate center staff do not try to influence the businesses. They do basic planning and control activities that authorize major decisions by the management team. Example activities would include accounting, controlling, and legal.
Value-adding role	The corporate functions work to add value to local businesses, e.g. leveraging corporate resources across businesses, facilitating synergies, or giving guidance. Example activities might include marketing, supply chain, procurement, HR, treasury, and communications.
Shared services role	The shared service functions are dedicated, customer-responsive, and performance-driven organizations, sometimes operating as separate companies or outsourced. Example functions can include IT (helpdesk), HR (training), and legal (support).

quickly and more completely between regions as this would be critical once the new import-fighter brand was launched.

Working through these demands allowed the corporate center team to develop objectives against which they could build action plans to help drive the MWB agenda forward. These were:

● Coordinate and enable an innovation agenda to support the MWBs.

● Help the regional units effectively share customer insight and knowledge.

● Help the regional units build a high performance culture.

By the end of the center's cascade session the mood was good. The center personnel were happy with the objectives they had created and were committed to fulfilling them. The senior executives and business unit managers who had participated were also in a positive frame of mind, as they felt that the center would no longer be able to hide behind its governance role, and this would go a long way toward addressing the cynicism and sniping so often directed at the center. Now, finally, Jan felt that the pieces were in place to really start making progress.

[2] For more on these roles, please see Goold, Michael, Pettifer, David, and Young, David (2001) "Redesigning the Corporate Center," *European Management Journal*, Vol. 19, Issue 1, February.

Maintaining momentum

If you have managed the early stages of your MWB journey well, you will have created a lot of energy, first in the leadership team and then in the wider organization. But with the passage of time that energy may start to dissipate as things do not go exactly as planned, and MWBs appear easier to win on paper than in reality. Even the most inspirational of chats with the leader no longer has the same impact. You need results, not just more words.

This is a natural transition. The leadership team has in effect said, "Trust us, these are the right MWBs, and we are capable of winning them," and before too long people want some evidence that this is true. You may have even tied incentives to successful execution of the MWB plans. So the initial hope that you created now has to be supported with real results. This juncture, maybe 4–6 months after the kick-off event, is a particularly risky point in the journey. You cannot rush events to show results where it is not appropriate, but neither can you ignore the emotional needs of the organization to see that you are moving in the right direction. Creating some visible wins is very important. But be careful: while quick wins are important to maintain or regain momentum, they must not be "manufactured." Trust and honest dialog are cornerstones of the MWB approach and it is not worth sacrificing these for "victories" that are not real.

If you have personal doubts or uncertainties, this is not the time to show them. You need to appear confident and resolute. This does not mean being blind, of course; if some MWBs have stalled or need redirection, move quickly to get things back on track. To give a regular pulse of energy to the whole process, insist on regular reviews of your MWBs, using your own version of the "green, yellow, red" tracking system that Jan's team installed. And remember, if one of your teams has a victory, make sure everyone knows about it. Peer pressure can become a powerful source of fresh energy.

How is the journey progressing?

About every six months, starting six months or so after the kick-off, you should conduct a review of overall progress and the degree of change that has been achieved in the organization since the MWB journey began. Such a review might include interviews with the kick-off event participants and members of the MWB teams, together with questionnaires sent to a wider group throughout the organization. (If you used an outside facilitator for the session, it can be helpful to ask her or him back to support this process.) The questions that you discuss in your interviews and ask on the questionnaire should allow you to assess progress in the areas indicated in Tables 7.2 and 7.3.

Table 7.2 Are we winning at the top?

Success indicators	Failure indicators
● MWBs drive the overall strategic agenda.	● MWBs not aligned with strategic agenda; objectives not reflected in plans and budgets. ● Lack of clarity and too much complexity.
● Visible commitment of leader and management; they speak with one voice, actions match words .	● Lack of ownership and dedication for follow-up. ● Different behavior outside and inside meeting.
● Leadership team is acting as a team, with shared objectives, openness, and trust. ● Team reinforcing each other on new ways of working.	● Unclear accountability roles. ● Still collection of individuals. ● Lack of support and recognition from others.
● Quick moves and early wins generate credibility for MWBs. ● Sense of urgency evident.	● Exclusive focus on short-term objectives. ● Initiative overload; poor prioritization.
● Progress measures are in place for all MWBs. ● MWB follow-up is built into existing management processes. ● Leader insists on new behaviors. ● Ability to get conflicts onto the table and resolve them effectively.	● Short-term targets absorbing energy and focus. ● Lack of progress measures and integration with core processes. ● Leader does not deal effectively with individual behavior. ● Daily workload allowing little "quality time" to think and change behaviors. ● Failure to accept failure (blaming others).

When you have the feedback, you should be able to determine overall progress and identify specific factors that are promoting progress (enablers) and those that are getting in the way (barriers). You can then take action to support and enhance the enablers, and reduce the barriers.

At the same time, the leadership team should use the results to "look in the mirror" and challenge themselves on how well they are living up to their commitments. At this point you should be able to see not only what is working in the organization and what is not, but also who in the organization still owns and drives the agenda established at the kick-off event, and who does not. Again, use what you learn from the review to take action that will accelerate the progress of your journey.

Table 7.4 Are we winning in the broader organization?

Success indicators	Failure indicators
● MWBs seen as important across the whole organization.	● Many people cannot articulate what MWBs are or what they mean for the organization.
● Ongoing communications helping to engage the organization.	● Communications sporadic and unfocused; at worst, not credible.
● Action priorities are clear.	● Staff do not understand what actions they need to take.
● Cross-division, cross-functional, and cross-geographic co-operation significantly improved.	● Confusion over who should be doing what. ● Continued competition for resources and budgets.
● Clarity of roles.	● Many competing priorities. ● Confusion over what is most important.
● Obvious personal commitment to the MWBs.	● Lack of commitment to the MWBs.
● More openness and trust.	● Strong resistance to any changes. ● Control culture and lack of risk taking.
● Morale is high.	● Top management to blame. ● Low energy levels.

Jan and his team decided to hold regular progress reviews of their overall journey that quickly became known as the "where are we now" sessions. Rather than focusing directly on the level of detail implied in Tables 7.3 and 7.4, however, the facilitator conducting the interviews started by asking a series of more general questions shown below. The resulting conversations were usually very rich.

1. Where are we making the most progress, and what are the main drivers of that progress? Separate internal and external factors. Identify successes that can be shared across the organization.

2. Where are we making the least progress, and what are the factors that seem to be causing us problems? Again, separate internal and external factors. Also identify lessons from failures that are useful to communicate more broadly.

3. More generally, are we working together more effectively than before the MWB journey began? Give positive and negative examples.

4. Specifically, has behavior at the top changed? Again, give examples.

5. How are we doing at lower levels? Has behavior changed – are we working more effectively across silos? Again, give examples.

6. Are the MWB teams working together well?

7. Are we following up effectively?

At the six-month point, these questions elicited a wide range of responses – and some sharp disagreements – on how things were going, driven perhaps by the fact that many of the respondents were under intense pressure to get the MWBs up and running, and were involved in the painful job of stopping the must-stops. Some of the interview comments were as follows:

> There is a lack of definition in terms of responsibilities and structures; and sometimes a conflict between the overall MWBs and the supporting battles we have to win at my level.

> We see clear pressure from HQ on 'make Q1 or else!' – there is an inability to say no and prioritize.

> We are still fighting internal battles much too much, rather than focusing on customers.

> Everyone's own sphere of influence still predominates. It is difficult to reach a common view.

> I have the impression that the group is not very keen to push my battle.

By the one-year mark, things were starting to look – and feel – better to almost everyone. As Jan considered the feedback, it was clear that all the effort they had put into communications and promoting teamwork was starting to pay off:

> There is more trust. And getting to know each other better has helped teamwork.
>
> Clear goals and milestones for our MWB have been discussed and agreed with the countries. We are now all working together.
>
> The key driver in my humble opinion is that the people in management have finally started to 'let go' and make people throughout the organization more responsible and accountable.

However, Jan also discovered during the one-year review that while the overall journey was definitely moving forward, there was not as much progress being made on one of the battles as he had previously thought. It was time to refocus that battle, re-energize the team running it, or maybe – worst-case scenario – abandon it.

Reaccelerating battles

Even with the best planning and follow-up mechanisms in the world, MWBs don't always move forward as intended. Sometimes the causes are internal, such as conflict between departments for scarce resources or a slowness to act when speed is of the essence. Or the problems may be external, the entry of an unexpected competitor into a key market or development of a "leapfrog" technology that leaves you at a disadvantage.

Once you establish that a battle requires remedial action, your first task is to determine what the problem is, and then to dig deeper to find out what is causing it. Your first step should be to revisit the detailed MWB action plan with the MWB team and other business unit members involved in the implementation. As you gather information you need to focus, as always, on both the intellectual and emotional sides of the issues, especially if you think the problem may be internal. What you need to sort out is whether there have been major external discontinuities that have thrown your initial analysis into disarray, or whether the real problems are internal and whatever you hear about external problems is just an excuse to cover up internal failures.

You may conclude that a major external event, such as the acquisition of a major customer, a technological breakthrough, or the imposition of new government regulations, is of real significance. If so, you will need to re-examine your previous analysis and decide whether there is still likely to be a big payoff from winning this battle, whether or not it is still winnable, and what it would take to refocus the battle to cope with the changed circumstances. Sometimes, you simply need to abandon a battle that has become obsolete or impossible. This is not failure, but pragmatism. Making tough choices is part of the job and it is better to use scarce resources and management time on battles that are winnable rather than squander them on those that are not.

making tough choices is part of the job

However, you may discover that the root cause of the problem is inside your organization. Common problems include:

1. Faulty initial planning, e.g. major challenges were underestimated, or your capabilities were overestimated.

2. Poor prioritization of critical activities, e.g. the MWB action plan was a laundry list, without focus, and no one knew where to start.

3. Misalignment, e.g. the supporting battles of different business units are not well aligned with the overall MWB agenda.

4. Overload, e.g. some must-stops have not been stopped, so team leaders simply don't have the time, energy, or resources they require to push the battle forward effectively.

5. Obstruction: some key players are not on board – their actions (or lack of action) may be overt or covert, but they are definitely slowing progress.

Once the internal barriers to progress have been identified, a recovery plan needs to be activated. If your issue is obstruction, the actions may have to be driven from the very top, especially if senior people are at the heart of the problem. Heads may have to roll, or at a minimum leadership positions in the MWB reallocated. If such extreme actions are required, take them quickly, because if you are slow to address such problems, it sends a dangerous signal to the organization. All of your communication and action to this point has emphasized that the MWBs are the top priorities for the organization, so you need to ensure that they are treated as such, not just at the outset, but throughout the journey. Removing managers who are blocking progress should also move you a giant step toward building a team that truly functions as a team.

We have emphasized the importance of visibly celebrating success. It is equally critical that you quickly address lack of progress. Your actions in each case will send loud and clear messages about your priorities throughout the organization. In fact, your willingness to replace top people who are obstructing the journey will probably send the loudest message of all.

Winning and moving on

As your journey progresses, there will come a time to declare victory on some battles and move on to the next ones. The basic tests of victory are the extent to which the battle is meeting its targets and whether it still needs the frequent attention of the leadership team. The Rubik battle described by Unilever executive Kees van der Graaf in the next chapter is a good example. This was a cost-centered battle and once the cost targets were achieved, the team moved on to new priorities. This did not mean that costs no longer mattered, of course, but the new ways of working that resulted from the cost-focused MWB had become part of normal operations, and the issue no longer needed the special attention of an MWB team.

Declaring victory is one side of the equation. The other is recognizing that new battles are required. New challenges and opportunities will always emerge as the MWB journey moves forward; that is the world we live in. The natural forum for debating and agreeing new battles is the team meetings during which the progress of the existing battles is reviewed. As you discuss what is changing in your external environment, and what new capabilities the organization is developing, the question of new MWBs will naturally arise. It is rare to go back through the full Phase One process to launch a new battle, however, because new battles tend to be launched one at a time, so the majority of the MWB agenda is already clear and underway. In addition, the team should be functioning well by now, so the commitment process to the new battle should be faster than when you were debating a full slate of battles with a collection of warring executives at the kick-off event.

This is not to say that new MWBs should not be subjected to the same rigorous testing and challenges as the original battles. Every new battle must meet the criteria we discussed in Chapters 1 and 5: impact, market focus, specificity, excitement, and winnability. They also need to be evaluated in terms of impact on the overall agenda, to ensure each new battle can be fought successfully, in parallel with the others that are ongoing. Equally, you need to listen attentively to the voices that might not yet agree on the battle – informed debate remains critical. The whole team needs to commit to the new battle.

Jan's team agreed quite readily when it came to declaring their first victory. Huge strides had been made in the first nine months in fixing the quality problems at the Belgian plant, customer satisfaction was steadily improving, and the salesforces in neighboring markets were no longer complaining about the level of returns. Jan felt there was now a strong team in place in the plant and everyone was confident they were on track. No longer did senior people have to call the plant every other day to deal with problems, as had been the case during the first three months. It was a clear win.

However, the team were in a far from congratulatory mood when their attention turned to the UK. Two big supermarket chains had adopted a new packaging technology and it was decimating sales of their leading product line. Profits were declining and everyone felt that the new technology could quickly spread to the rest of Europe. Boris, the head of R&D, shifted uncomfortably in his seat as he outlined the basis of the innovation that threatened them – the bottom line was that they had to catch up fast, but it would not be easy. Some of the other team members had made pointed remarks about missing trends and it was clear that the team were moving back toward silo thinking. Jan had to step in and make it clear that they had to look forward – not blame each other for the past. And they had to launch a new battle. After several hours of debating the issues and potential courses of action, the group gave their commitment to move forward. The European packaging MWB was added to the agenda – and Boris would lead it.

Driving success: going the last 10 percent

We could not believe it. It was a pleasant surprise that he was going to attend our event anyway, as we are a small part of the company in a remote location, and then when we heard his house had burned down the previous day, we just assumed he would not be here. But he showed up! People were overwhelmed. That single act did more than anything else to convince not just us, but the whole organization – because the rumor mill was on to the story within hours – that the CEO was serious about the new agenda.

As must be clear by now, there is no such thing as a "perfect" MWB journey. There will always be ups and downs that will challenge the leader and the entire organization. Our experience, having watched many leaders in action, suggests that a large part of the success is about "going the last 10 percent," doing small but critical things that may be personally challenging but matter immensely. Like the CEO who showed up the day after his house burned down.

There is no comprehensive list we can provide of these activities or moments, but you will recognize them, often after the event! Because your "last 10 percent" actions are likely to be instinctive, and not planned to create the impact they do. And sometimes they will become turning points. One divisional manager whose unit had fractious relations with a powerful union, upon hearing that one of his hourly people had been injured, drove overnight to the hospital to visit the injured worker, and as it turned out was at his bedside before the union representative showed up. (And the union rep lived in the town where the hospital was located.) That simple act, unpremeditated, fundamentally changed the balance of power between the union and that company.

Other examples relate to dealing with friends. Very often leaders of the MWB agenda have friends in the organization who are not quite on board, or not quite up to dealing with the challenges that the new agenda presents. Many leaders are tempted to ignore those realities and live with what one senior manager labeled "satisfactory under-performance." It is not blatant, but everyone recognizes it. If you are going to go the last 10 percent, you deal with it. You act humanely, but you act.

Often the last 10 percent factors are not dramatic moves, however, but just day-to-day small actions that cumulatively make a large impact. Communication, for example, is always important, and never more so than in the vulnerable stages of an MWB journey, when momentum is slipping and people are questioning the whole initiative. As the leader, you have a symbolic role to play and everything you do, for better or worse, is magnified a thousand times. So even though you are tired, you need to make that last phone call or have that difficult face-to-face conversation. Do not send an email instead, or ask someone else to deal with it. It is not the same. Go the last 10 percent.

Jan looks forward

Eighteen months after the kick-off event Jan felt that the European MWB journey was going "pretty well," and he felt more than ever that it was the right thing for his organization. He knew they still had a long way to go, but he and his team were getting more and more comfortable with the new ways of working, and results had definitely improved. Even US head office executives were asking about this "must-win battle thing" and were clearly wondering whether they should introduce the approach in other parts of the world.

Jan paused to reflect on what he had learned about leading an MWB journey, and what he thought he needed to concentrate on going forward.

1. It's all about energy and focus

I knew from the outset that the major challenge would be to create energy and focus, and that is something that never really goes away. Even now, a year later, I am amazed to discover people in the organization who still don't really "get it." I have communicated what we are doing and why so often I am getting bored with my own speeches, but obviously I can't stop yet. In the next year I have to make sure that we keep celebrating our successes, and deal with the remaining foot-draggers. It is a carrot and stick thing. There are great rewards for all of us as we win our battles and I have to make sure there are consequences for individuals who do not join the team. I have probably moved too slowly on the consequences side.

As for me personally, I always have to remember that I am in the spotlight every day. "Walking the talk" is not an empty phrase, and everyone is watching to see if I am doing it. One false move from me – a wrong decision, a slip of the tongue when I am tired – could set us back six months.

2. People make the difference

I know it has been said in almost every management book ever written, but going through an experience like this really makes you realize just how true it is: people do make the critical difference. Choosing the right people to lead the MWBs is vital – I made one mistake there – and then you need to manage the interface between them and the traditional silo leaders. The underlying philosophy is to give people the responsibility and resources they need to get the job done, and then hold them accountable for results. Easy to say, but always more difficult to do in an organization full of interdependencies.

The Americans often talk about capturing the hearts and minds of their people and I never paid much attention to the phrase, but now I see what they are getting at. To get people fully on board we have used both intellectual arguments and given opportunities for emotional involvement. The reality is that some people lead with their heart, others with their head, but if you work hard on both sides of the equation, as we have done, you should be able to capture most of the people, most of the time.

3. **It is more than winning individual battles**

   My managers have a natural tendency to focus on the shortterm and the MWBs that involve them most directly. But a major objective of our MWB journey is to build a successful organization for the future, not simply to win a series of (admittedly important) battles. Again this is easier said than done, when demands for improved earnings are staring managers in the face every day. So balance between the short-term wins and the long-term development of the organization is critical and it is my job to ensure that we get it. It is not "either or," we have to do both. Win the battles *and* build the organization for the future.

As Jan turns to the list of calls that need to be made before he goes home that evening, we leave him feeling that this organization of the future is really starting to become a reality. A good point at which to hand over to Kees van der Graaf who can take up the tale from further along the MWB journey route. Like Jan, he has been through ups and downs, reaching the point after two years with Unilever Ice Cream where real change and success is making a positive impact on business results.

e i g h t

From tent to tent: the Unilever Ice Cream journey

This chapter describes a two-year MWB journey that was undertaken by the Unilever Ice Cream Frozen Foods business group, as told by Kees van der Graaf, the Unilever executive who led the journey.

Even before I took over our European ice cream and frozen food division in April 2001, I knew we had a problem. An employee survey showed that the people in the business felt it was lacking in strategic focus at the top. Apparently one day, leadership was banging on the table and saying, "We will launch a product everywhere, with the same brands, the same proposition," and the next day you would see one person doing one thing, another doing something else – no one was working as a team. There was no shared agenda, as every country manager was doing his own thing.

The second shock for me in that survey was the conclusion that the organization was not a place where it was safe to speak up. Speaking your mind about the real issues was not welcomed, and it was not an environment where risk taking was encouraged. Making matters worse, there was little trust between the country operations and the center, or between the countries themselves.

It was then that I decided we should be the first Unilever business to embark on an MWB journey. Unilever's Executive had begun their own leadership journey the year before and management had decided the divisions should do the same thing. I thought it was exactly what we needed. Even though our financial results were acceptable, I thought they would not stay that way for long. We had to change the status quo – and the sooner the better.

Kees van der Graaf

Born in 1950 in Goes, The Netherlands, Kees van der Graaf studied mechanical engineering, followed by business engineering, at the University of Twente, The Netherlands.

In 1976 he joined Unilever as a trainee and rose steadily through the ranks, working in a variety of Unilever companies in Europe and the US. In April 2001, Kees became president of the Ice Cream Frozen Foods business group. In May 2004, he was elected to the boards of Unilever PLC and N.V. and appointed Foods Director. In February 2005, he was appointed as President, Europe for the combined companies, with effect from April 2005.

Kees is married with three sons, all studying in Amsterdam. He loves sailing, golf, gardening, and skiing. During the Christmas holidays you can find him in the Swiss Alps. He avidly supports Feijenoord and the Dutch national soccer team.

Kees is founder and chairman of two charity organizations which raise funds for muscular dystrophy research. Both charities have contributed significantly toward finding a cure for this disease.

The kick-off event: engaging the team

I decided that we would invite about forty-five people to the kick-off event. My objectives were to understand more about the business and the issues it faced, while at the same time establishing myself as the leader. I also hoped we would arrive at a shared set of strategic priorities. So, up to a point, the more people who were there the better.

Before the event, I read a lot: the division's strategy, its operating framework, its magazines. I also had chats with a lot of people. I knew some of them already, but I did not know them in their current jobs. So I saw these talks as vital, as I needed to know what people were thinking about the business and each other. This is also very much my style: in my view a leader has to listen to and be interested in the people in the organization. I liked the fact that during the kick-off event we would tell each other our "lifelines," and put all the taboo topics on the table for discussion. If we were going to succeed together, we had to develop trusting relationships.

The final step before the event was to work with a facilitator, walking through the program that had been proposed by the central group, and modifying it to suit my objectives. I had to make sure the program focused on our needs, and was not just some standardized head office-mandated process.

Our kick-off event was held in an old chateau in the French countryside. There was no one else around, no fancy facilities, no formal meeting rooms, no place for PowerPoint presentations. The location was ideal for getting to know each other, putting difficult issues on the table, making choices, and building the basis on which we would work together for the next few years.

The night before the event began, we had dinner with one of Unilever's two chairmen, who talked about what was happening in our overall business and the importance of the journey on which Unilever as a whole had embarked. He emphasized that this journey focused on both our businesses and our people. He emphasized a quote that came from another executive: "How could we have such talented executives producing such mediocre results?" This was what we were there to address in the days and years ahead.

Day 1: opening personal windows – the tent incident

On the first morning, we walked together through a wood to the ruins of a castle and there we started talking. It was my first real exposure to the group as a whole and I didn't know what to expect. We began talking about our "hopes and fears" for the business. It was a strange environment for this discussion because you could feel in those ruins what had once existed around us, and you could see what had become of it. Ice cream was a business in which Unilever had long been a leader. Would we lead it to new levels of success or would we be responsible for its ruin? As we slowly pulled away from the site in some old buses, the chairman was watching us. It was almost like he was saying, "It's now over to you."

Our next stop was a small village. Here we sat and talked about our "myths and taboos" and how we as a leadership team operated and handled conflict. These discussions took place in small groups, and as each group turned in summaries of their discussions, I could see the real issues were already coming out. Then we walked on and suddenly arrived at a large Turkish tent prepared for us, which of course no one expected. This became the scene for a very important interaction. The group kept saying to me: "There isn't a strategy, there is no clarity about rules and responsibilities, it is all lacking." "But," I said, "I've read the strategy you wrote a few months ago; it was even signed by the European board members individually" (all of whom were in the discussion). I added pretty strongly: "Do you always sign documents you don't agree with? If you do so we will have a problem, because this is something I find unacceptable."

Well, they found it unacceptable for me to say that. The result was a fierce discussion with the group saying, "who are you, thinking that you can say those things to us?" and me saying to them, "if you are the kind of people who sign documents and then don't live up to the commitment you've signed, I will have great difficulties." After these emotional outbursts we moved to a cautious peace, and a decision to have lunch and go back to it later. During lunch, we had some light entertainment, but no one was paying real attention anyway. We were all thinking about the incident in the tent. After lunch we agreed that we had to go back and reflect upon why it had happened.

Afterwards, everyone referred to the "tent incident" as the point that change started to happen. I explained why I was angry, why I don't allow people to sign documents that three months later they say they can't remember and haven't lived up to. In my value system, a commitment is a commitment. And if you don't want to commit, you speak out and you don't commit, and I won't make you a member of the team that is supposed to be committed. But if you do commit, I expect you to deliver against your commitment. My explanation helped the group understand why I was so disappointed with the reaction I got. Did I have second thoughts about challenging the group so directly just a few hours into my tenure? No, it happened spontaneously. The only thing I regret is the strength of my response.

At the end of the day, we did an exercise referred to as "personal lifeline" which led each of us to talk about who we are as individuals and some of the formative experiences in our lives. I went first, and whereas the others did it in small groups I did mine in front of the entire group. It was a frightening prospect – talking about myself, my private life, my drivers, even though I am very proud of the situation at home and the things I am doing beyond my job. I was nervous, but I liked the environment. It was informal and safe: people were lounging on sofas in a big circle, and there was nobody from outside. So I felt comfortable, even though it was a risk, being publicly exposed. I always get emotional in such situations and people feel that. By the end I felt like I had run a marathon – I was physically and emotionally exhausted. But that first day set the tone for the whole event. As the leader, you have to be totally honest and authentic; people know when you are acting.

Day 2: opening windows on the business

That open and trusting tone continued the next day as we started with an exercise called "business lifeline" in which we drew our views of where the business had come from and where it was today. The picture that emerged was mass confusion (see Figure 8.1). We had no shared understanding of where we had been or where we were. We each

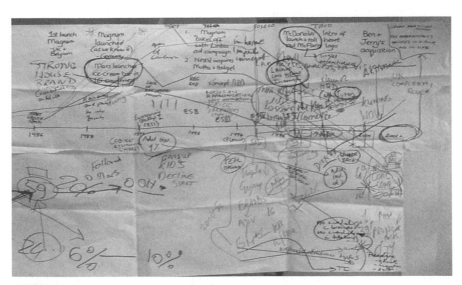

Figure 8.1 Ice Cream Europe business lifeline

looked only from our own perspective and we were obviously in different worlds. The only thing we agreed was that the launch of Magnum (a major ice-cream brand) was a high point, and that was a long time ago. The other point of alignment was the question mark at the end of the lifeline. We were clearly at a transition point but no one knew which way the business was going to go.

Our next exercise was to look at the business from the outside-in, taking the perspective of customers, consumers, and competitors. We covered the walls of an entire room with our market data and previous analysis. We didn't debate the data, we focused on understanding it and building a common view of where we were today. As we took the perspective of major competitors it was fascinating to see the passion with which our people identified with the new emerging competitors that were threatening our business, and the bureaucratic feeling that overtook the group when they took the perspective of the major players that were similar to us. You could sense the excitement and passion that must have been in our business years ago, which was now gone.

Later that day we started to build a shared view of the business we wanted to create, using a simple visioning exercise, "looking back on our success." What struck me was that this was the first time the group had ever talked about what they wanted the business to become, and how they wanted to work together as a leadership team. It surprised me enormously that such discussions had never taken place. Until then, strategy had been quoted at them from the top. Now they were creating it. The strategy exercise that I challenged them about in the tent had been artificial; it never had these interactions. The whole notion of values was completely new to them too. That came as a real shock. So we began to develop values together, and to decide which behaviors we wanted to promote and which we wanted to stop.

Day 3: colliding to decide on our must-win battles

The next day was a mixture of analysis and emotion, as we moved from "what kind of business we want to become" to identifying the key battles we had to win to get there. We began in small groups and then had to bring it all together, which meant getting forty-five people to agree "these are our five key challenges and we will give them priority in our decision making and resource allocation." Reaching general agreement on the main themes was not difficult, but forcing the group down to five priorities certainly was. But we had to do it. If you have ten battles there are too many escape routes. I would rather have just a few, and be clear that they are not a permanent set of activities. These are battles to win a war, and battles must be short, sharp, and quick. The time horizon should not be longer than two years. If the targets are too general or too far away – some of the things on our original list were more strategic objectives than battles – then there is not enough of a sense of urgency.

Days 4–5: committing to one agenda

Priorities only lead to action when they are understood, shared, owned, measured, and monitored. So during the last two days we created a more detailed understanding of what we meant by each MWB, the key issues we would have to address, and the measures we would use to track progress. Most importantly, we also chose the people who would assume responsibility for leading each battle. We purposely selected country company chairmen as the MWB leaders. Suddenly, managers who had only been looking out for the interests of their country had a shared, collective task. In an instant, we made holes in some thick silo walls. We needed a regional perspective to succeed in Europe, and these appointments were a major step in that direction. We created a team of interdependent leaders.

Toward the end of the session, we again discussed how we would work together, identifying the behaviors we would accept and not accept, and what each of us would do to support our new agenda. The key questions were: "What am I going to do differently from now on? What are the priorities that I am going to set for myself? What will I do more of, and less of?" These commitments were stated aloud, so everyone could hear what the others had committed to.

As our final act together at the offsite, I wanted us to create a physical symbol of our new commitments. So we mounted a large piece of paper on a board in the middle of the room and said, "If you are committed, put your name and a message on that board. And if you are not committed, you can have a chat with the HR people, who will find you another job in or outside Unilever." This was a shock: it had never been done before. I was saying either you are with us as we try to change this business, or find another job. It made a huge impact. I still remember the first person who stepped forward to put his message up. Then, almost like an avalanche, the rest just jumped to the board to write their messages. Everybody committed, and there were some very powerful messages. We hung the board in our main boardroom for the next two years as a constant reminder of our commitment.

Figure 8.2 Our commitment board

Preparing to return home

The kick-off event was a success, and I think that was for three reasons. First, it was tailored to our particular challenges; it was not a generic design. Second, the group was the true, extended leadership team of the business, not just a head office group. Third, and most important, we set an open and honest tone early in the program and maintained it. We went from an atmosphere of "it's not safe to speak out here" to "it is very safe to speak, because the only thing that matters is that we are going to crack these business issues."

No one thought for a second that what we had agreed to would be easy to achieve. We were going to ask our people, and ourselves, to think and act differently – to be open to new ways of working and to build an environment of trust and interdependence. It would be a challenge for our entire organization. In my own mind, I kept going back to the chairman's question: "Why are such capable people producing such mediocre results?" We were all capable, and we could no longer accept this situation.

As we prepared to return home, I was excited. We had a clear and aligned agenda – an agenda I loved and a level of ambition I liked. It reflected a level of business behavior that inspired me. I also felt that I now knew the team and had established my leadership. But I was worried as well – there was a lot of work to do and it was not a clean ship, but we had made a good start.

Getting out of the organizational swamp

As I had a brief sabbatical before fully engaging in my new job, I returned to the office about one month after our MWB kick-off event. I quickly realized that not a lot had happened during my absence, and there again seemed to be a lack of strategic clarity. People had created action plans to support the MWBs, but for some battles the action plans were an endless shopping list – I don't exaggerate when I say hundreds of actions. I quickly came to the conclusion that we needed to do something to get things moving.

From market dive to action plan in Barcelona

We decided to focus on one critical battle on which little progress had been made. I believed that the basic problem was that our executives did not really understand the marketplace realities that surrounded this battle. Our people often spend time in our markets, but usually they focus primarily on our products and activities, not taking a supplier, consumer, or competitor view. To win the MWB in question, we needed a fresh look. It was not a question of doing better what we were already doing, we needed a whole new approach.

So we decided to start this event not in a meeting room but rather with in-depth "market dives" in five major European cities. We created five teams and each visited a city for two days, focusing on one of five themes associated with the MWB. After these "market dives" the fifty executives involved came together in Barcelona to share their experiences and learnings. The insights were profound – and crystal clear. We were too expensive and our margins were too low, not because of pricing but because our costs were too high. There was no need for a long debate, it was clear.

What was also striking was the passion that these executives displayed when they shared their stories and photographs from their market visits. They were energized and excited about what they had seen and the opportunities they had identified. They spent the next three days redefining our action plans for the MWB. The long wish list disappeared, replaced by a concrete and prioritized list of things that we needed to do immediately to win this battle. The decisions made during those three days led to some of our biggest victories in the following year and a half.

One of the priorities that came out of this session, for example, was the need to drastically reduce our cost base. It was quickly decided that we would:

- Cut the number of stock-keeping units (SKUs) by 50 percent.
- Reduce the number of ingredients by 50 percent.
- Rationalize our supplier base, cutting the number again by 50 percent.

We did not carry out detailed analysis on these targets. The need was obvious, and debating and justifying financial details would have slowed us down. We adopted them on the spot, and once we had agreed, they were not negotiable. Within ten days we had freed up a multidisciplinary team to take on the challenge. They had a clear mandate from the top and buy-in from the entire executive group.

Rubik, as this project was known, yielded €42 million a year in cost savings, as well as much improved operational effectiveness because of reduced complexity. Why did it work? Because the mandate was clear, there was active leadership and support from the top, and full agreement throughout the organization that it needed to be done.

Other victories also flowed from the Barcelona event and our fresh market-based approach sent some clear messages to other MWB teams about what it might take to succeed in their MWBs.

Focusing the leadership team: commitment means accountability

The Barcelona session was very satisfying, but the bigger challenge I faced after our kick-off event was to focus the attention of the leadership team, and then the entire organization, on the MWBs. I realized that I had to embed the MWBs into all of our meetings, processes, plans, budgets, reviews, and systems. The MWBs had to become the primary agenda for our leadership team every time we met. Everyone had to realize that these MWBs would not go away and that never again would we all sign a strategy document and then put it aside and forget about it. From now on I would hold everyone accountable for progress against each of our MWBs, and that accountability implied consequence.

In spite of the promises made during the kick-off event that we would operate as a co-ordinated, European-wide business, it was clear that accepting interdependence was going to be easier in theory than in practice. Our country leaders had built their careers making their own decisions, and leading local teams. Working together across boundaries did not come naturally, but it had to happen. So at every meeting I insisted that we assess our progress on each MWB, and this repetition made it clear that I believed that the primary role of the leadership team was to ensure victory in the MWBs.

My other challenge was to clearly communicate and get buy-in to the MWBs throughout the organization. If we were going to win our battles, we needed the understanding, ownership, and commitment of the entire organization. The question was how to do it.

Making it happen: engaging the organization

2002 cascade: communicating the MWBs

Every year Unilever has a "cascade event" at which our most senior executives report on the progress of Unilever overall, and then the business units take an additional day to discuss their own issues. I decided that the annual cascade would be a natural place to review our MWB agenda every year with our top 150 people, highlighting the progress, or lack of progress, that we were making.

Our first Ice Cream and Frozen Food cascade was in Amsterdam, in 2002. It was in an old ship's engine factory, a strange and provocative setting, with all the cranes still in place – we wanted people to think differently. The first topic on the agenda was complexity. Our business was simply too complicated, and we needed to drive that message home to everyone. So as the event was starting we dropped 5000 packs of our food products from the ceiling. It worked – the effect was dramatic. The falling products made a lasting impression, and everyone got the point. We were running a business that was too complex, with too many products, too many different SKUs. We then started debating some of our "hot topics." We set it up like the British Parliament, and people had to advance and defend statements, in such a convincing way that others would join in. If not, their proposition would be rejected. We discussed five or six topics extremely well – people got physically, emotionally, and intellectually engaged. And we ended up with a clear understanding of where we stood on some key issues and made some decisions that brought more focus and attention to those issues.

The third thing we did was to re-examine our values and behaviors. We had begun to address values and behaviors during our kick-off event, but we needed to do more. We started with the core values we had previously defined, and began to identify the behaviors needed to support them. It was a very long list to start with and we made it shorter and shorter, until we ended up with a few specific acceptable and unacceptable behaviors. This was the starting point for the event that we held six months later in Spain.

Motivating 1200 people: "how the rest was won"

In the following months we continued to make progress on our MWBs, and the 150–200 most senior managers were now truly engaged. However, to succeed we needed people from across the organization to understand what we were doing and why, and what they needed to do to ensure our success.

To do this, we planned an event that would involve 1200 of our managers from across Europe. We had never done anything involving so many employees, and there was resistance to the idea from the very top of the company. Why spend the money, what would be the direct benefit, and so on. But for me there was no question that we needed to directly involve this larger group if we were going to move forward.

The event had three broad objectives. The first was to get the group excited about the array of new products we were introducing. We couldn't rely on traditional word-of-mouth communication and documents. We needed people to have hands-on experience with the products in a mass setting to feel the excitement of what we were creating.

The second objective was silo busting. We still had far too many independent kingdoms. These silos had to go. We needed everyone to see that the creation of a Europe-wide business would benefit us all, and would allow them to be more focused and successful in their markets. The third objective was to focus on behaviors we had identified in Amsterdam as being necessary to support our values. We needed people to understand that we expected new ways of operating – from both them and their bosses.

When we informed the 1200 people of the meeting, we did not tell them where they were going or what they were going to do. This led to a lot of speculation and excitement. "Has Kees gone completely crazy?" was a question many were asking. When everyone arrived in the remote area of Spain that we had chosen for the event (on chartered planes to reduce cost), we had a huge welcome party that celebrated the launch of our new Heart Ice Cream brand identity and the progress we were making as a business. After dinner people moved to the bullring for a light show and to experience the new brand identity for themselves.

The following morning we drove in a long row of buses to a village that had been used to make spaghetti western films. It was staffed with cowboys and Indians who welcomed us and gave us a show. We then gave the group the instructions for the day: "You will receive a brief that will tell you which value (and associated behavior) your group has to demonstrate through a film. In making your film, you will have to write a text, train yourselves for the stunts, rehearse, learn to do the make-up . . . everything – all within a day!" We had arranged costumes for everyone and the themes were assigned – each theme was one of the acceptable or non-acceptable behaviors we had agreed in Amsterdam.

So they had to act out the values. In the end we had forty teams working on these behaviors. We had real TV crews to film them and during the night we made it into one big movie: "How the Rest Was Won." The following day we screened it for all 1200 people. It was a total surprise – one and a half hours of beautifully put-together, well-edited material. It made a huge impact, seeing the forty different acceptable and unacceptable behaviors expressed in this way. The groups did a great job of getting the messages across. We will never forget what the values are or what they mean. We will also never doubt what we can accomplish in a short period of time if we all work together.

During the filming, we arranged for the entire village to experience our products. We focused on our Knorr brand and the different meal opportunities it could provide – learning from around the world. There were cooking sessions with Knorr products, and Knorr-based snacks were available. We had talks on frozen food as a method for maintaining food freshness. Our products and product experiences were everywhere anyone went. It was a total immersion in what we as a business were attempting to develop and offer to our consumers.

During this event we also launched a program called "Caring for the Future of our Children." Why did we do this? My conviction is that managers are more effective both for the company and for themselves if they do something for the world in which they live. It comes from my own experience working with charities for disabled children, which has brought me a new perspective on life; to see how rewarding it is to meet people you otherwise never would have met, and to understand how little it really takes to make a positive difference.

What we did was quite simple. We gave everyone a day off to do something for children in their local communities. We didn't prescribe what. The aim was for people to understand that the issues were closer than they realized – in all the areas where we have operations there are many children in need of help, not just the handicapped. Our initiative was undertaken under the umbrella of Unilever's sixth thrust for 2010, "engage with communities and environment."

Overall, the Spanish event was very important. Some 1200 people experienced the new brand, the new food, and the values. When people left they were very excited about the direction we were taking. They were becoming part of our team, owning and living our common agenda.

2003 cascade: accelerating momentum

The day before our 2003 cascade event we held a press day in Rotterdam to demonstrate our progress to the outside world. We issued a press release celebrating the launch of our revised brand identity and announcing our commitment to invest in ice cream as a strategic business in Unilever. We also distributed booklets about the new direction Unilever was taking with ice cream. We followed this up with forty-eight press interviews in six hours. It was a bit like the way the car industry does it, showing some prototypes, without giving guarantees that they would ever reach the market. But we showed what a fantastic product ice cream is. We gave them curry ice cream, cheese ice cream . . . you name it! It was all there! At the same time we launched our Heart fashion line, with a catwalk and mannequins showing off new beach clothing.

However, while we were enjoying success in parts of our business, we were also losing market share in some important areas. So we decided that the theme for this cascade itself would be "accelerating momentum," and we asked the leadership group to look in detail at our progress in each MWB. Instead of looking internally at progress against budgets, however, they were to look from the outside-in. Were we keeping pace with the rate of change in our markets? Were we leading our markets or playing catch-up? How could we accelerate our actions and build momentum in the market? The end result was that we stepped up our pace, not so much on the overall battles but on the supporting must-wins behind each of them.

We also used this cascade event to look at the progress we were making in our "Caring for the Future of our Children" program. We found that there were initiatives in every community in which our people lived, led by a volunteer or HR person. An internal website had been set up (not management's idea, but from the bottom up) to exchange ideas and information. The results were fantastic. Not only did the communities benefit, but our people felt the difference. They were more motivated; their eyes were opened; everyone became a better marketer because they understood why they were doing it. The message we all took away was that we are here to stay; we are going to shoulder our responsibilities and solve the problems that need to be solved.

From tent to tent: two years on

During my final year of leading the business, we had to maintain our focus and momentum, as well as focus on some MWBs where we were still not making sufficient progress. For one MWB we repeated the market dive approach we had taken in Barcelona. Again, we involved executives from across the organization, and again it worked.

Other battles had essentially been won, and it was time to replace them with new emerging challenges. My own leadership challenge this year was to keep the organization inspired and focused. The journey was still ongoing, even though in two years we had achieved a lot.

In September 2003, to showcase our progress, we arranged for a number of investors and analysts to visit our innovation center in Rome. It was a pretty dramatic move, but there had been a lot of criticism of ice cream, and we wanted to fight back. Analysts had been making comments like: "Why is Unilever in ice cream? Why is Unilever in frozen foods? They should just sell frozen foods and focus their ice cream business on the areas where they are doing well and just forget the rest."

We wanted to show them that ice cream is a category where you can make profits, indeed very good profits. We had moved from an erratic profit performance, largely influenced by weather, to a situation with a much lower breakeven point. Even in a bad weather year our profit performance is much more even. The most important thing was to demonstrate that, financially, ice cream was an attractive business for Unilever.

Our second objective was to show that we had a full innovation funnel that would excite the market. We showed them around the center and had interactive sessions – like nothing they had done with us before. They experienced for themselves the elements of the new Powerbrand, the innovative flavors, the scooping experiences, the making of shapes. They could see what we were doing with the new cabinets for the market – the storage spaces for the ice cream were not just for storage, but were a display unit to attract customers.

The event was a very important step in rebuilding investors' confidence in Unilever, and in Unilever's ability to build the ice cream business. At the end, a number of them commented that this was the best "touch and feel" event they had participated in. Our most outspoken critic even took the microphone at the end of the event and expressed his positive reaction in front of everybody. The feedback after the session was entirely positive, but the message was also: "We've seen and believe in what you're doing, and we would like to see it work in the market. Now you've got to deliver."

This was a perfect statement of where we were. We had developed the strategy and the products we needed to succeed. We had the organization and the people in place. We were beginning to see success in the markets. Our entire organization was focused and working hard. But the task was far from done.

2004: celebrating success, preparing our future

The 2004 cascade event was time for celebration. We had just achieved a record year in all aspects of the business (helped by a fantastic summer in Western Europe): highest ever profit, big progress in getting growth back into our business, lowest overheads, lowest number of SKUs, Heart brand launched, and our factory restructuring programs nearly completed. An enormous number of milestones had been met.

The 2004 cascade would be my last with this business. By coincidence this event, like my first, was also held in a large tent, but this time in the Austrian mountains. We chose Austria for a number of reasons. To start with, our business in Austria had been sponsoring the Austrian ski team, the most successful in the world, for the past three years. This team was working with our local company, participating in our TV spots, being there when we launched a cooking group, cooking with us, sharing our important events, and supporting press launches. The result was that the Iglo brand had become the most popular brand in Austria, even more than Coke! And finally, the Austrian company had exceeded its targets three years in a row, so it was a great location for celebrating success.

We also wanted to re-energize our Caring for the Future of our Children program. So we decided to launch "Heart for Kids." It was a better title and captured the feeling that we wanted to get across. And we found there was an SOS Children's Village nearby for orphaned refugee children that needed €20–30,000 to close a gap in their budget. But we did not want our people to write out checks. We told them: "You've got to raise that money yourself." So they organized all sorts of creative fund raising events and raised an incredible €190,000 – an Olympian achievement versus the original target.

For the event itself we developed a Winter Olympics theme and divided our people into teams that included the SOS children. We then did the weirdest sports you can think of: sports balloons, throwing snowballs, sledge-riding, and of course racing the Austrian downhill team. Between and after the events people were walking around the tent sharing their successes and all teams were encouraged to take ideas home to try for themselves; in some cases using the examples they had just heard to define a "must-do" plan to accelerate the roll-out of key projects. The event clearly built motivation for our MWBs, but also made sure we kept our focus on the environment around us. Even in the midst of discussions of success people got the message that a lot of work still needed to be done.

A leader's personal perspective

Personally, these last few years have affected me in a dramatic way. Unilever is a very complex company and that complexity can make you bureaucratic and slow, when you need to be fast. But I have realized that you can get diverse multinational teams coming from a mind set of being independent market leaders – "we know how to do it" – to a way of working where it *is* possible for them to think and act in an interdependent way. Moving the thinking to: if I do something well others can benefit; if others have done something well, I can use that. For me, this was always a dream. Just by focusing on involving our people, helping them work together to build a shared perspective, by having them develop the agenda and then holding them accountable, we were able to achieve a lot.

The organization changes that took place in the late 1990s were, in all honesty, probably not enough, both at the Unilever corporate level and in my unit. In hindsight, I should have been more forceful on some things, particularly in dealing with individuals who reverted to "local," independent attitudes and slowed things down. So while the organization was becoming faster, it was still not fast enough. And it had become simpler, but not simple enough. People knew the rules of engagement, but they still tested the borders. So decisions and corrective measures were required, but even done gracefully people disappearing swiftly would have made a bigger impact.

Perhaps the biggest organizational improvement is that people now "expect and accept" a leader to take the lead. You are allowed to make mistakes, if you are prepared to learn from and share those mistakes with others. Beyond that, the way the different parts of the organization work together has changed dramatically. The formerly independent fiefdoms are now thinking and acting in an interdependent way that few would have thought possible two years ago.

On a personal level, I feel that I have definitely developed as a leader. I trust my gut more than ever before. Just like the senses in your fingers or your eyesight, your gut is also a way of sensing. And if it tells you not to do something, or indeed to do it, just trust and go for it. On the other hand, my biggest weakness is probably that I am still pretty impatient. If I see the direction we should take, but the organization is hesitating, I do it myself. I don't wait for others. The moment that a decision is made that this is what we are going to do, for example on Rubik, I don't accept "no" for an answer any more. It needs to happen. I help the team by taking away the barriers, including people, and facilitating action.

But my impatience goes against establishing a strong organization. So now when I see where we should go, I try to take the organization by the hand and go there together in a harmonious way. You continually need to reinforce focus and accountability. You bring people along then by being open and honest, inspiring them, and by being energetic. Trust your people, and give them freedom, but make sure it is within a well-defined framework.

My other learning is that we have got great people throughout the organization to whom you can give more responsibility than you may be inclined to, early in their careers. And if you create a team – a real team – of average people, you will be much better off than if you work with a collection of brilliant individuals. We have great people at Unilever and when we let them play as a team, we are unbeatable. We have great values; they come from the heart. They are honest. They are truthful. A successful company in today's world cannot be artificial.

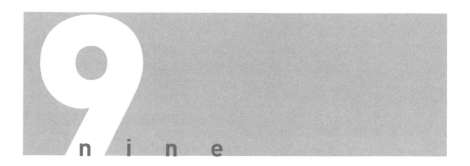

Where do you go from here?

If you have read this far, you have probably decided that the MWB concept and the idea of a MWB journey would add value to your business. If this is true for you we would suggest that you revisit the questions highlighted at the ends of Chapter 1 and Chapter 3.

Even if you are not completely convinced that a MWB journey is right for you, we hope we have given you food for thought. Our aim is not to add to the collection of business books on your shelves, but to highlight some core principles that you can apply to the challenges that you face every day:

1. Knowing where you are going will never be out of fashion. And in a rapidly changing environment, knowing your desired destination is more important than ever. Even though your route will change more than once, every business, every person, needs to know what they are striving for.

2. Strategy-making matters, but not just as an intellectual process. It is a journey, with a team, that evolves and changes as your business environment shifts and competitive advantages erode. The most powerful competitive advantage, if you can sustain it, is a strong team that works well together.

3. You have to insist that your organization makes tough, informed choices about the few battles that you really do need to win. And collectively, your portfolio of battles should move you toward your ultimate objectives, both short and longer term.

4. To win, you will probably need to work across the silos in your organization, and create a climate which will bring out the power of diverse managerial perspectives. Transparency and honesty must be valued. The people who will act should be the people who decide. The team should be driving, not driven by a lone leader.

5. Your way forward should be both aspirational and inspirational – not only to the team making the choices but to the broader organization. You need to tap into both the intellectual and emotional energy that will drive collective ownership, actions, and the behaviors that support winning.

6. To turn your strategy into actions that will bring victory in the marketplace, it must be backed up by good reporting, accountability for collective results, and consequences – both positive and negative.

7. Throughout the journey, the tenacity and courage of the leadership team will be tested, more than once. To win, you will need strong emotional and intellectual commitment.

Good luck. When you embark, enjoy the journey!

index

234